A SHORT GUIDE TO
EQUALITY RISK

SHORT GUIDES TO RISK SERIES

Risk is a far more complex and demanding issue than it was ten years ago. Risk managers may have expertise in the general aspects of risk management and in the specifics that relate directly to their business, but they are much less likely to understand other more specialist risks. Equally, Company Directors may find themselves falling down in their duty to manage risk because they don't have enough knowledge to be able to talk to their risk team in a sensible way.

The short guides to risk are not going to make either of these groups experts in the subject but will give them plenty to get started and in a format and an extent (circa 100 pages) that is readily digested.

Titles in the series will include:

- Climate Risk
- Compliance Risk
- Employee Risk
- Environmental Risk
- Fraud Risk
- Information Risk
- Intellectual Property Risk
- Kidnap and Ransom Risk
- Operational Risk
- Purchasing Risk
- Reputation Risk
- Strategic Risk
- Supply Chain Risk
- Tax Risk
- Terrorism Risk

A Short Guide to Equality Risk

Tony Morden

Routledge
Taylor & Francis Group

LONDON AND NEW YORK

First published 2011 by Gower Publishing

Published 2016 by Routledge
2 Park Square, Milton Park, Abingdon, Oxon OX14 4RN
711 Third Avenue, New York, NY 10017, USA

Routledge is an imprint of the Taylor & Francis Group, an informa business

British Library Cataloguing in Publication Data
Morden, Tony, 1946-
  A short guide to equality risk. -- (Short guides to
  business risk series)
  1. Diversity in the workplace--Management.
  2. Discrimination in employment--Prevention. 3. Equality.
  4. Risk management.
  I. Title II. Series
  658.3'008-dc22

Library of Congress Cataloging-in-Publication Data
Morden, Tony, 1946-
  A short guide to equality risk / Tony Morden.
    p. cm. -- (Short guides to business risk)
  Includes bibliographical references and index.
  ISBN 978-1-4094-0450-7 (pbk) -- ISBN 978-1-4094-0451-4 1. Discrimination
  in employment. 2. Diversity in the workplace--Management. 3. Labor laws
  and legislation. I. Title.
  HD4903.M67 2010
  658.3008--dc22

                                                    2010048034

ISBN 13: 978-1-4094-0450-7 (pbk)

Contents

List of Figures

Acknowledgements

I wish to acknowledge the contribution of the following people to the development of my understanding of the complex, and sometimes controversial subject described in this Short Guide: Susan Haider; Tony Hutchinson; Harvey and Jim of the West Midlands Police; Jasvinder Sanghera; and Neil Stevenson of the Law Society of Scotland.

I must also record my sincere thanks to Dahlia El-Manstrly who acted as a researcher for this project, and to Marion Fisher who prepared the final documentation on my behalf.

Introduction

The purpose of this Short Guide is to look at the risk that is associated with the formulation and implementation of the Equality, Diversity and Discrimination (or "EDD") Agenda. The Guide usually refers to this as "EDD Risk" for reasons of brevity. Powerful and well-resourced Agendas for Equality, Diversity and Discrimination are now widely established in Western democracies, particularly where these countries possess a multicultural or a polyglot character that results from past imperial history (as in the UK, France or The Netherlands), or from extensive involvement in foreign trade, or from policies that actively encourage immigration (as in the case of the USA and Canada).

Concepts of EDD Risk are, for very good reasons, well established in such societies. Failures of compliance with Agendas for Equality and Diversity, or worse, incidences of Discrimination, Victimisation or Retaliation are increasingly seen as unacceptable, whether from a political, social, legal or medical viewpoint. The risks of failures of compliance are escalating, be it in terms of cost, the potential for damage to reputation, or the potential for loss of government or public sector contracts.

This Short Guide describes Equality, Diversity and Discrimination (EDD) Risk in two arenas, those being: (i) of employment; and (ii) of the service environment. This approach mirrors a typical focus of government policy in the West.

The subject material of the book is arranged sequentially. Each chapter has an Introduction and then concludes with a Postscript. The Postscript recaps the main points of the chapter. It then anticipates the content of the next, thereby assisting the flow of the text. The actual content of this Short Guide is schematised in Figure I.1.

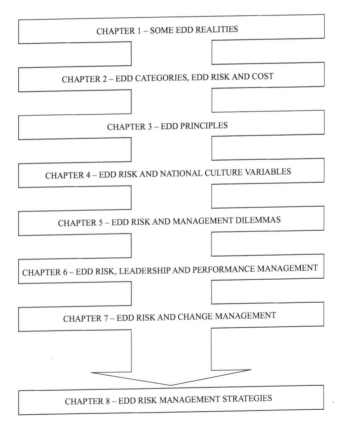

Figure I.1   Content of this short guide

The source material which forms the basis of this Short Guide is acknowledged in any one of four ways, as follow:

- by reference to the author's two core Ashgate management texts cited in the Bibliography; or

- by reference to key EDD sources cited in the Bibliography; or

- by direct reference in the text; or

- by reference to internet sources to be found in the Public Domain and cited as 'Internet PD'.

Finally, the author must state the obvious caveat that where an individual or an organisation decide that, after reading: (i) any part; or (ii) all of this Short Guide, they are in need of further information about specific EDD issues or specific EDD Risk that directly affects them, they must seek appropriate professional, trade union, legal, medical or medicolegal advice.

Tony Morden,
North Yorkshire, UK, 2011
www.equalityrisk.com
www.principlesofmanagement.com

per cent of company board members. The percentage only exceeds 20 per cent in Sweden and Finland; it is below 5 per cent in Malta, Italy, Cyprus, Luxembourg and Portugal. Company boards are defined here as the "highest decision-making body" and the location of responsibility for the processes of corporate governance described in later chapters of this Guide (source: EU).

Gender pay gap – there is a persisting gender pay gap in the EU. This gender pay gap (defined as the difference between men's and women's average gross hourly earnings as a percentage of men's average gross hourly earnings) is estimated in 2007 at 17.4 per cent on average throughout the EU. The gender pay gap, however, exceeded 20 per cent in seven countries and 25 per cent in two countries (source: EU).

Welcome on board? – many of the post-1945 Asian and Caribbean immigrants, and successive generations of their children (who are British citizens by birth), have been victims of entrenched and sustained discrimination in the UK.

Sacked for being gay – a Turkish referee who was sacked for being homosexual is fast becoming an icon of the gay rights movement, said Nicholas Birch in *The Independent*. Halil Ibrahim Dincdag, a 33 year old from Trabzon, had been officiating in his local league for 13 years when he was outed by Turkey's football authorities and relieved of his position. Dincdag subsequently appeared on television to discuss the case – 'an act of considerable courage' in a country where homophobia is rife. Turkey's most popular football commentator believes Dincdag should not be reinstated. 'I reckon [he] would have a tendency to give more penalties to good-looking, tough footballers', viewers were told (source: *The Week*, 4 July 2009).

The case of the "wee poof" – Jonah Ditton, a highly successful Scottish media sales manager, was sacked by C.P. Publishing of Glasgow because he was gay. Subsequent action at his Employment Tribunal resulted in the payment of £120,000 in compensation for discrimination by his former employer on the grounds of Jonah's sexual orientation.

On the day after he started his new job, Jonah's boss commented on a blue tie that he was wearing. On being told that the tie was by Hermes, his boss replied 'Oooh, Hermes' in a camp voice. Several days later, Jonah alleged that his boss asked him if he was from Stoke-on-Trent, which is rhyming slang for "bent". When he wore a cream-coloured suit to work, his boss told him that he looked like a "cream puff". On the day that Mr Ditton was sacked, he had attempted to join in a light-hearted discussion about marital relations but was told by his boss to 'shut it, you wee poof'.

Mr Ditton was phoned that evening and sacked, after only eight days in the job, on the grounds that he was not 'psychologically balanced'.

Mr Ditton commented that his sexual orientation had never been an employment issue before working for C.P. Publishing and stated that it had no bearing on his ability to do his job (source: Internet Public Domain (PD)).

Lawry's restaurants to pay $1 million for sex bias against men in hiring – the US Equal Employment Opportunity Commission (EEOC) announced (2 November 2009) the settlement of a sex discrimination lawsuit for $1,025,000 against Lawry's Restaurants Inc. for allegedly pursuing a long-standing company policy of refusing to hire men for food server (waiter) positions in violation of the Civil Rights Act of 1964 which prohibits sex-based discrimination (source: Internet PD).

Helen Green wins court victory – Helen Green, a female employee of Deutsche Bank in London, was awarded £800,000 in damages in a landmark UK 2006 workplace bullying case. Ms Green was subjected to a 'relentless campaign of mean and spiteful behaviour designed to cause her distress' that led to serious problems of mental health disability on her part and a subsequent inability to work at her former level of employment. Ms Green claimed that she had been subjected to 'offensive, abusive, intimidating, denigrating, bullying, humiliating, patronising, infantile and insulting words and behaviour' and was subject to crude and lewd comments from her former male colleagues (source: Internet PD).

Regal Entertainment Group to pay $175,000 for sexual harassment of male employee by female co-worker – Regal Entertainment Group, a US movie theatre chain, will pay $175,000 and furnish significant remedial relief to settle a federal sex discrimination and retaliation lawsuit filed by the US Equal Employment Opportunity Commission (9 November 2009). The EEOC had charged that the company subjected a male employee to sexual harassment by a female co-worker and then retaliated: (i) against him for complaining about the unlawful conduct; and (ii) against two supervisors who tried to help. In its lawsuit the EEOC charged that a male employee at a Regal theatre in California was subjected to sexually hostile behaviour by a female co-worker who repeatedly grabbed his crotch. When the male victim and his supervisor complained to the theatre's general manager, she failed to take adequate steps to stop or to prevent the harassment. Instead, the EEOC alleged, she retaliated against the harassed employee and against the two supervisory employees who had tried to assist in resolving the situation. The retaliation took the form of unwarranted disciplinary action, unfairly lowered performance evaluations and deliberately strict scrutiny of performance (source: Internet PD).

Switalski v F. & C. Asset Management – in early 2008, Gillian Switalski, a senior legal executive at F. & C. Asset Management claimed that alleged sexual discrimination, harassment and victimisation (retaliation) had left her unfit to fulfil her role. The Central London Employment Tribunal upheld this claim and plans to sue her former employer for substantial compensation were announced. The claim arose after Ms Switalski left her £140,000 per year job in September 2007 after her manager criticised her for choosing a flexible working pattern which was designed to help her care for her two sons, one of whom had cerebral palsy and the other who had Asperger's syndrome. Ms Switalski's manager was shown to have a particular difficulty in working with women and in appreciating the reasons for Ms Switalski's requests for flexible work (source: Internet PD).

Japanese restaurant to pay $30,000 to settle EEOC pregnancy discrimination suit – a Japanese restaurant will pay $30,000 and furnish other remedial relief to settle a federal pregnancy discrimination lawsuit filed by the US Equal Employment Opportunity Commission (16 November 2009). The EEOC had charged that Tepanyaki Limited of Utah had discriminated against Alison Woodbury by firing her because she was pregnant. Ms Woodbury had been employed as a waitress but during her initial training the restaurant's manager discovered that she was pregnant and terminated her contract (source: Internet PD).

Healthcare company settles EEOC disability discrimination lawsuit – St John Health System Inc. of Tulsa, Oklahoma will pay $100,000 and furnish other relief (18 November 2009) to settle an EEOC lawsuit alleging a breach of the Americans With Disabilities Act by failing reasonably to accommodate a hearing-impaired operating room scrub technician (source: Internet PD).

Mental health – The UK charity "Mind" comments of mental health disability that 'we've all done it. Called someone crazy, a nutter, weirdo, paranoid. But behind the names there's a weight of ignorance and abuse that crushes people with mental illness ... the hard truth is that 1 in 4 of us in the UK will experience a mental health problem at some point in our lives'.

A World Bank international study of mental illness in 2000 found that it was second to heart disease as the greatest disability among employees. By 2010 it is expected to have reached the number one position.

The UK campaign "Time To Change" comments that 'employment can promote good mental and emotional well-being, but can also act as a trigger for mental health issues. Whether you have existing mental health issues or not, long hours, sustained pressure, poor management and difficult working relationships can all take their toll on mental health. Three in ten employees will have a mental health problem in any given year, yet fewer than one in ten employers have a mental health policy to help staff sustain good mental health.

In a survey commissioned in 2006, over 40 per cent of employers thought that none of their employees would be dealing with any form of mental ill health, even though statistically speaking one in four (UK) employees may (suffer) mental distress. The lack of awareness amongst employers can be seen as part of a vicious circle. People with mental health problems don't want to disclose this to their employers for fear that there might be repercussions. This acts as a barrier to seeking support and requesting workplace adjustments (available from the provisions of the Disability Discrimination Act 1995). As a result, employers can be reluctant to believe a mental health problem might be an issue in their workplace.

Employers are often concerned that acknowledging mental health problems in their workforce will lead to additional expense. However, this is not necessarily the case – by putting relatively inexpensive preventative measures in place an employer can avoid hefty costs down the line due to sickness absence. There is an assumption that illness is incompatible with work but with the right help, people experiencing mental health problems can – and do – stay at work. The Chartered Institute of Personnel and Development (CIPD) has shown that a quarter of UK workers describe their mental health as moderate or poor, yet 98 per cent continue to work regularly, showing that there is a real need for all workplaces to be better equipped to manage mental health problems' (*Time To Change Update,* Issue 5, Winter 2009/2010).

US service corporations to be sued for religious discrimination – the EEOC announced (2 November 2009) that it would sue Administaff Inc. and Conn-X LLC as joint employers of brothers Scott and Joey Jacobson whom, it alleged, had been subjected to verbal and physical harassment because they were Jewish. The EEOC asserted that beginning in 2005 and continuing throughout their employment the Jacobsons were called 'dirty Jew', 'dumb Jew' and subjected to anti-Semitic behaviour by managers and co-workers (source: Internet PD).

May the Force be with you? – the Canadian media has of recent years shown keen interest in the behaviour of some members of the Royal Canadian Mounted Police (the RCMP). For instance, one of its senior officers was described in a Maclean's Report as 'an old-school military guy, abrupt, rude, a real straight talker. He barked orders. He swore like a sailor' (source: *Maclean's*, 2007, vol. 120 no. 34).

An RCMP constable of First Nations origin was told by his superior that 'natives are worse than white trash and are low-lifes, gas sniffers, women abusers and drunks' (source: *Occupational Health & Safety Canada*, 2006, vol. 22 no. 8).

Another constable took stress leave due to workplace conditions that he claimed were rampant with harassment, racism, bullying and physical intimidation. 'I was being called names that I had never heard before. I started being ashamed of not being white' (source: *Maclean's*, 2007, vol. 120 no. 46).

An RCMP Superintendent came under fire when civilian workers complained about his harassment, inappropriate language and unacceptable behaviour (source: *RCMP Watch*, 2008).

Also, a female constable complained of harassment because she followed the rules. 'It's been nothing but a nightmare', she said. 'I followed the policy, I followed every proper procedure, dealt with every proper step I was supposed to do, and I'm the only one that's seen as, not necessarily a bad guy, but just someone that they'd rather not have dealt with' (source: *RCMP Watch*, 2008).

Bank teller fired for being 'too old' – Bellco Credit Union has agreed (13 November 2009) to pay $57,250 and to furnish other relief to settle an age discrimination lawsuit filed by the EEOC, resulting from the dismissal in 2003 of a 61-year-old bank teller at a Bellco branch in Colorado (source: Internet PD).

"Crumble" – the author's elderly mother, who lived on the south coast of England, became so ill that she needed hospital treatment. As her doctor tried (in the author's presence) to arrange her admission, it rapidly became clear that the hospital authorities on the other end of the telephone were describing her as "crumble". This appears to be a derogatory term used by some people in the UK National Health Service (NHS) to describe a patient who is elderly and in poor health. Pointing out that his mother had been paying her taxes for many years and was entitled by right to proper healthcare, the author then ensured that his vigorous protestations about the insult to his own mother had the effect of drawing matters rapidly to a close; an ambulance with a cheery crew appeared soon after.

SOME UGLY

Disability hate crime – which was brought into sharp focus by the UK case of Fiona Pilkington, who burned herself and her 18-year-old disabled daughter to death in a car after suffering a sustained hate campaign by local youths during 2007. The 2003 Criminal Justice Act defines such hate crime as being motivated by prejudice or hatred towards another person who is in some way disabled. The UK's "Disability Now" campaign's *Hate Crime Dossier* lists an appalling record of savage crime against the disabled, whether they suffer from physical or sensory impairment, learning difficulties or autism (source: Internet PD).

Homicide – workplace stress leading to harassment is a major cause of workplace violence in the USA. Actual homicide (murder) is a leading cause of fatal occupational injury, particularly in the case of women. The San Francisco Gender Equality Principles Initiative, for example, asks private sector corporations to ensure the safety of women workers by:

- prohibiting or preventing all forms of violence in the workplace, whether verbal, physical or sexual; and

- ensuring the safety of female employees in the workplace, in travel to and from the workplace, and on company-related business.

POSTSCRIPT

This chapter has given some practical examples of the implementation of the Equality, Diversity and Discrimination (EDD) Agenda.

The chapter has also given some illustrations of the variety and complexity of the EDD Agenda. It has shown the seriousness of some of the issues associated with that Agenda, and the nature of the risks to which implementation failures may give rise.

This Short Guide now moves on to Chapter 2. That chapter describes the key features of the EDD Agenda and illustrates the various statutory and duty of care responsibilities associated with it. It categorises the different generic types or groups of people to whom the EDD Agenda is applied, such as women, members of ethnic minorities or the disabled, etc. And it analyses in detail some of the risks and costs associated with a failure properly to understand and to implement that Agenda.

(2) EDD Categories, EDD Risk and Cost

The second chapter of this Short Guide analyses the concepts of Equality, Diversity and Discrimination that make up the EDD Agenda. The chapter describes some of the categories (or groups) of people to whom there is likely to be a statutory or duty of care responsibility, and against whom discrimination in employment and in service provision is likely to be unacceptable or illegal. It outlines the typical scope of the application of equality enactments. It summarises some of the forms of discrimination that are commonly to be found in the employment and service arenas, and it describes various types of EDD Risk and Cost.

THE EQUALITY AND DIVERSITY CONCEPT

The first purpose of any equality and diversity legislation is *to manage diversity and to promote equality and opportunity*. Key features of this concept are summarised in respect of the employment and service environments as follow.

Equality – the concept of equality is concerned with ensuring that people are not discriminated against unfairly, but are instead given *the same and equal opportunities*. The Law Society of Scotland (LSS) states, for instance, that 'equality is about creating a fairer society where everyone can participate and has the same opportunity to fulfil their potential. Equality is backed by legislation designed to address unfair discrimination based on membership of a particular group'. The UK Equality Act 2010 notes in this respect 'the desirability of reducing socio-economic inequalities' and calls for the exercise of functions identified in the Act to be made 'with regard to the need to eliminate discrimination and other prohibited conduct', such as harassment and victimisation.

Diversity – the concept of diversity involves *the valuing and respecting of difference*, whether this difference (for example, race, disability, gender, etc.) is visible or not. There is a need to recognise that people are not all the same and that they have different but equally valuable life experience, knowledge and skills to offer. The Law Society of Scotland states that 'diversity is about recognising that everyone is different in a variety of visible and non-visible ways. It is about creating a culture and practices that recognise, respect and value difference. It is about harnessing this potential to create a productive environment in which the equally diverse needs of the customer/client can be met in a creative environment. It is about creating a workforce who feel valued/respected and have their potential fully utilised in order to meet organisational goals'. The LSS suggests that the main features of the concept include the recognition of difference, the linking of diversity to business goals, the perception of diversity as a "mainstream" value and an emphasis on the benefits of diversity. The UK Essex County Fire and Rescue Service (ECFRS) states in this respect that it is working towards achieving a diverse workforce that reflects the character of the community it serves and provides a service that meets the needs of all sections of that community.

STATUTORY, "GENERAL", "DUTY OF CARE" AND "EQUALITY DUTY" REQUIREMENTS

A variety of United Kingdom (UK) statutory, general, duty of care, and equality and diversity requirements are listed as follows.

The "General Duty" laid down in the UK Equality Act 2006 – is that of 'encouraging and supporting the development of a society in which:

- people's ability to achieve their potential is not limited by prejudice or discrimination;

- there is respect for and protection of each individual's human rights;

- there is respect for the dignity and worth of each individual;

- each individual has an equal opportunity to participate in society;

- there is mutual respect between groups based on understanding and valuing of diversity and on shared respect for equality and human rights'.

The UK Commission for Equality and Human Rights (CEHR) – is placed under a duty to:

- promote awareness and understanding of the importance of equality and diversity, and to protect people's rights in these matters;

- promote awareness, understanding and protection of human rights;

- promote equality of opportunity;

- promote awareness and understanding of the various rights conferred by the equality enactments;

- enforce the various equality enactments by ensuring compliance therewith;

- work towards the elimination of unlawful discrimination;

- work towards the elimination of unlawful harassment;

- encourage good practice in relation to equality, diversity and human rights.

More generally, the UK Commission for Equality and Human Rights is placed under a duty to work towards the elimination of prejudice against, hatred of, and hostility towards people categorised as protected "groups" by European Union legislation and by Paragraph 10 of the UK Equality Act 2006. Paragraph 4 of the UK Equality Act 2010 subsequently describes these groups or categories as having "protected characteristics". The protected categories are described in the next main section below.

The Public Sector Equality Duty laid down by the Equality Act 2010 – states (Paragraph 149) that a public authority must, in the exercise of its functions, have due regard to the need to:

- Eliminate discrimination, harassment, victimisation and any other conduct that is prohibited in respect of persons who are categorised as having protected status.

- Advance equality of opportunity between persons who share a relevant protected characteristic and persons who do not share it.

- Foster good relations between persons who share a protected characteristic and persons who do not share it.

The Act also decrees that a person or an organisation (such as a sub-contractor) that is not a public authority, but nevertheless exercises public functions, is also bound by the same Equality Duty.

THE PROTECTED CATEGORIES OF EUROPEAN UNION AND UNITED KINGDOM EQUALITIES LEGISLATION

There are, at the time of writing, at least nine protected groups or categories of EU and UK Equalities Legislation. These categories are listed as follow in alphabetical order.

1. *Age* – legislation may outlaw age discrimination in employment and vocational training, but not at the time of this writing, in the provision of goods and services (such as life insurance-type products or certain types of

medical treatment) in the UK. The Equality Act 2010 currently states that person "A" does not discriminate against person "B" under the heading of Age where A can show that A's treatment of B is 'a proportionate means of achieving a legitimate aim' (Paragraph 13 Section 2).

2. *Disability* – which is defined as a physical or mental impairment that has a substantial and long-term adverse effect on the ability of a person to carry out day-to-day activities. This category (*inter alia*) covers discrimination in employment, the provision of goods and services, and the role of qualifications bodies and trade organisations. The Equality Act 2010, Paragraph 15, states of disability discrimination that 'a person (A) discriminates against a disabled person (B) if: (i) A treats B unfavourably because of something arising in consequence of B's disability; and (ii) A cannot show that the treatment is a proportionate means of achieving a legitimate aim'. It then states a caveat that this provision may not apply where A shows that he or she did not know, and could not reasonably have been expected to know, that B had the disability.

3. *Gender reassignment* – by which protected status is afforded 'if a person is proposing to undergo, is undergoing or has undergone a process (or part of a process) for the purpose of reassigning the person's sex by changing physiological or other attributes of sex'. In this respect 'a reference to a transsexual person is a reference to a person who has the protected characteristic of gender reassignment'.

4. *Marriage and civil partnership* – by which a person is protected if he or she is married or is a civil partner.

5. *Pregnancy and maternity* – the Equality Act 2010 consolidates women's work-related rights in respect of pregnancy and maternity leave. This protected characteristic also applies to the provision of services and public functions, premises, education and access to membership associations. Paragraph 17 adds that a woman who has given birth must not in any respect be treated unfavourably if she chooses to breastfeed her child. Paragraphs 73 to 76 then reinforce the protection in the specific respects of: (i) the calculation of pay and remuneration; and (ii) the calculation of benefits accruing from the membership of, and contribution to an occupational pension scheme whilst the woman is away from work as a result of pregnancy or maternity leave.

6. *Race* – discrimination in employment and in the provision of goods and services is prohibited on the grounds of a person's race, colour, nationality and their ethnic and national origins. Racism in general terms consists of words, practices or conduct that disadvantage (or instead advantage) people precisely because of race, colour or their ethnic and national origins. Paragraph 9 of the Equality Act 2010 notes in addition that 'a Minister of the Crown may by order amend this section so as to provide for caste to be an aspect of race'.

7. *Religion and belief* – discrimination is prohibited on the grounds of religion, religious belief and philosophical belief (or any lack thereof). This relates to employment, vocational training and the provision of goods and services. Some religions may also be covered under the race category where they can be "mapped" to a specific ethnic group (for example, Sikhism), in which "combined discrimination" based on "dual characteristics" may be held to occur (Equality Act 2010, Paragraph 14).

8. *Sex or gender* – discrimination in relation to employment and in the provision of goods and services is prohibited on the grounds of a person's gender.

9. *Sexual orientation* – discrimination is prohibited in employment, training and the provision of goods and services on the basis of a person's sexual orientation (or perception of it; or an association with someone with a perceived orientation) towards persons of the same sex, persons of the opposite sex or persons of the same and of the opposite sex. For example, the overt homophobia described in Chapter 1.

EQUAL PAY FOR WOMEN

Equal pay for women is an issue that arises from the fact of pay inequality between men and women. It is often introduced into domestic politics in developed countries as an economic and social problem that needs government intervention via regulation. Generally, and for cultural or religious reasons, the degree of pay disparity in third world countries is much higher. However, there are some societies where women earn more than men; according to a survey on gender pay inequality by the International Trade Union Confederation, female workers in the Gulf State of Bahrain can earn 40 per cent more than male workers, while female presenters in the US media may be in the process of overtaking the earnings of their male counterparts (source: Wikipedia).

Morden (2004) notes that pay discrimination takes place 'where, for no good reason, employees are recruited, paid and promoted on the basis of their sex. Similarly, discrimination may be evident where there are separate employment policies for men and women. Discrimination may take the form of:

- The reserving of some jobs for men or women only.

- The offer of a lower level of remuneration for equal work. This has led to the development of the "equal pay for equal work" concept as a remedy.

- The offer of a lower level of remuneration for work of an equivalent value. This has led to the development of the "equal pay for work of an equal value" concept as a remedy, under which members of one sex may not suffer discrimination on the grounds of job content or equivalent value.

- The application to men and women of the same performance measurement standards when such standards are likely unreasonably to have the effect of discriminating against one sex more than another'. For example, the UK financial services sector where a significant proportion of income is based on performance-based bonuses or commissions. This is held to disadvantage women who have family responsibilities.

- 'A disproportionate allocation of promotion opportunities to one sex rather than the other'. In the case of women this may be referred to as the "glass ceiling".

In the case of the UK, the purpose of the Equal Pay Act 1970 was to remedy some of the incidence of discrimination indicated by the use of differential terms and conditions of employment between men and women. This legislation reflects the EU requirement for Member States to 'ensure and maintain the application of equal remuneration for equal work as between male and female workers'.

The US Equal Pay Act 1963 requires that men and women in the same workplace be given equal pay for equal work. The jobs need not be identical, but they must be substantially equal. Job content, not job title, determines whether jobs are substantially equal. All forms of pay are covered by this law, including salary, overtime pay, bonuses, stock options, profit sharing and bonus plans, life insurance, vacation and holiday pay, cleaning or gasoline allowances, hotel accommodations, reimbursement for travel expenses and benefits. If there is an inequality in wages between men and women, employers must not reduce the wages of either sex in order to equalize their pay.

Equal pay in Canada is regulated by the Canadian Human Rights Act 1978, by the Constitution Act 1982 which established the Canadian Charter of Rights and Freedoms, and by Provincial and Territorial Law. Canadian legislation distinguishes between: (i) "pay equality"; and (ii) "pay equity". *Pay equality*, or equal pay for equal work, refers to the requirement that men and women be paid the same if they perform the same job (for example, electrician) in the same organisation. Reasonable differences in relative pay may then in either case be permitted for reasons of merit or seniority. *Pay equity* means that male-dominated occupations and female-dominated occupations of a comparable value must be paid the same if they occur within the same employer. For example, if a hospital's nurses and electricians are deemed on whatever grounds to have jobs of equal importance, they must be paid the same. One way of distinguishing between the two concepts is to define pay equality as guaranteeing the rights of men and women as individual employees, while pay equity guarantees the rights of male or female dominated occupations as groups.

The UK Equality Act 2010 also deals with the issue of the assessment of whether work is of equal value. Paragraph 131 applies where a question arises during the proceedings of an Employment Tribunal 'as to whether the work of one person (A) is equal to the work of another (B), and A's work and B's work have been given different values by a job evaluation study' which has been deemed (that is, by the use of expert judgement about the facts) to be 'based on a system that discriminates because of sex, or is otherwise unreliable'. A job evaluation study is defined in Paragraph 80 as 'a study undertaken with a view to evaluating, in terms of the demands made on a person by reference to factors such as effort, skill and decision-making, the jobs to be done by some or all of the workers in an undertaking or group of undertakings'.

The UK Equality Act 2010, Paragraphs 77 and 78, then points out the importance to the resolution of pay inequalities in organisations of effective information disclosure. It proposes to make:

- A term of a person's work that purports to prevent or to restrict that person (P) from disclosing or seeking to disclose information about the terms of P's work unenforceable against P in so far as P makes or seeks to make a relevant pay disclosure.

- A term of a person's work that purports to prevent or restrict the person (P) from seeking disclosure of information from a colleague about the terms of the colleague's work unenforceable against P in so far as P seeks a relevant pay disclosure from a colleague, whether that colleague is current or from the past.

The Act also suggests regulations that 'may require employers to publish information relating to the pay of employees for the purpose of showing whether ... there are differences in the pay of male and female employees'. This "gender pay gap information" might have to be published on an annual basis.

UNITED STATES CATEGORIES OF EQUALITIES LEGISLATION

The US Equal Employment Opportunity Commission (EEOC) lists categories of US Employment Equalities legislation in alphabetical order as follow.

1. *Age* – the Age Discrimination in Employment Act (ADEA) forbids age discrimination against people who are aged 40 years or older. At the same time, it may be legal for an employer or other covered entity to favour an older worker over a younger one.

2. *Disability discrimination* – which is illegal under the Americans with Disabilities Act (ADA) and under the Rehabilitation Act which covers federal employees only. Employers and other covered entities may not treat a qualified individual with a disability who is an applicant or employee in an unfavourable manner because he or she has a disability.

    Disability discrimination also occurs when an employer or covered entity treats an applicant or employee less favourably because he or she has a history of disability (such as cancer that is controlled or in remission) or because he or she is believed to have a physical or mental impairment that is neither "minor" nor "transitory" (defined as lasting or expected to last six months or less).

The law also protects people from discrimination based on their relationship with a person with a disability (for example, AIDS), even though they themselves do not have any disability.

As in the UK, US law requires an employer to provide "reasonable accommodation" to a job applicant or employee with a disability, unless so doing would cause "undue hardship" (defined as significant difficulty or expense for the employer). The concept of reasonable accommodation (or "reasonable adjustment") is dealt with in later chapters of this Guide.

3. *Genetic information discrimination* – it is unlawful to discriminate against applicants or employees on the grounds of genetic information. The Genetic Information Non-discrimination Act (GINA) prohibits the use of genetic information in making employment decisions, restricts acquisition of genetic information by employers and other covered entities, and strictly limits the disclosure of genetic information.

   Genetic information is defined by the EEOC as information about an individual's genetic tests and the genetic tests of an individual's family members, as well as information about any disease, disorder or condition of an individual's family members (that is, an individual's family medical history). Family medical history is included in the definition of genetic information because it is often used to determine whether someone has an increased risk of getting a disease, disorder or condition in the future.

4. *National origin discrimination* – involves treating applicants or employees unfavourably because they are from a particular country or part of the world, because of ethnicity or accent, or because they appear to be of a certain ethnic background. National origin discrimination can also involve treating people unfavourably because they are married to (or associated with) a person of a certain national origin or because of their connection with an ethnic organisation or group.

5. *Pregnancy discrimination* – which means treating a female applicant or employee unfavourably because of pregnancy, childbirth or a medical condition related to pregnancy or childbirth. If a woman is temporarily unable to perform her job due to pregnancy or childbirth, or a medical condition related thereto, the employer or other covered entity must treat her in the same way as any other temporarily disabled employee, for instance, by providing modified tasks, alternative assignments or disability leave.

6. *Race or colour discrimination* – which means treating an applicant or employee unfavourably because he or she is of a certain race or because of personal characteristics associated with race (such as skin colour, hair texture or facial features). Colour discrimination involves treating someone unfavourably because of skin colour or complexion. Race or colour discrimination can also involve treating someone unfavourably because the person is married to a person of a certain race or colour, or involved with an organisation or group that is usually associated with people of a certain race or colour. The EEOC

notes in addition that an employment policy or practice that is applied to everyone, regardless of race or colour, could be illegal if it has an "indirect" negative impact on the employment of people of a particular race or colour even though it is not job-related nor is it necessary to the operation of the business. The EEOC gives the example of a "no beard" employment policy that is applied to all male employees. This may have a disproportionate impact on African-American men who have a predisposition to a skin condition that causes severe shaving bumps.

The concept of indirect discrimination is described in a later section of this chapter.

7. *Religious discrimination* – which means treating an applicant or an employee unfavourably because of his or her religious beliefs. US law protects people who belong to traditional organised religion, such as Christianity, Judaism, Islam, Buddhism, Hinduism or Sikhism. It also covers people who hold other sincerely held religious, ethical or moral beliefs. Religious discrimination may also involve treating someone differently because that person is married to (or associated with) an individual of a particular religion or because of his or her connection with a religious organisation or group.

The EEOC then notes that unless it would be unsafe or an undue hardship to the employer's operation of its business, the employer must reasonably accommodate an employee's religious beliefs or practices (such as the daily pattern of Muslim prayer). This reasonable adjustment might include leave for religious observance, flexible work scheduling, voluntary shift swaps or substitutions, job reassignments or modifications to workplace practices.

The employer is also bound to make a reasonable accommodation of dress or grooming practices that have religious significance. These, for example, might include the wearing of religious dress or head coverings (such as the Jewish yarmulke or the Muslim headscarf) or the adoption of certain hairstyles or facial hair (such as Sikh uncut hair, turban and beard, or Rastafarian dreadlocks). It also includes an employee's observance of a religious prohibition against wearing garments such as short skirts or trousers in the case of women.

8. *Sex-based discrimination* – which means treating an applicant or an employee unfavourably because of that person's sex or because of his or her connection with a group or organisation that is generally associated with people of a certain sex. An employment policy or practice that is applied to everyone, regardless of sex, may be illegal if it has a negative impact on the employment of people of a certain sex and is not job-related or necessary to the operation of the business. For example, the reserving of service-type activities to women even though there are equal pay policies in place, as described in Chapter 1.

OTHER PROTECTED GROUPS OR CATEGORIES

Anti-discrimination legislation elsewhere in the world may extend to any of the following.

"First Nation People" or people with aboriginal status – as in Canada and Australia.

Former prisoners with "spent" criminal conviction – against whom discrimination in recruitment is often reported even though:

- they have completed a term of imprisonment or punishment that resulted from conviction for a civil or criminal offence; or

- they have received a pardon for that offence.

Morden notes that 'different systems of employment law perceive this issue in different ways. Some will insist that the full biographical history of applicants for employment should, as a matter of principle, be revealed to the prospective employer and to the people with whom the appointee will work. Others perceive the matter from the viewpoint of necessity. Details of spent or completed convictions must be revealed if they are deemed to be materially relevant, for instance in the cases of jobs involving security issues, cash handling, confidential systems, or computer networks'. Such a policy might instead be applied to the sensitive circumstances associated with teaching or working with children or young people.

At the other end of the scale, some Canadian provinces, for example, normally prohibit employers from seeking any record of completed criminal conviction.

Marital and parental status – Morden notes that 'widespread discrimination takes place on an international basis in that married women are often regarded as a short-term employment prospect, and not worth the investment in training or promotion ... women may be expected to leave the workforce at the birth of their first child, and not to return thereafter. In more extreme cases, women could not undertake paid work without the written permission of their husbands.

Attitudes to what constitutes "discrimination" under this heading depends ... on cultural, social, and religious values about the role of women, and about how children should be brought up. Attitudes also vary towards "partnership" arrangements as opposed to marriage. Employers in some countries will recognise the maternity rights of married women, but not those of women in non-traditional, partnership, common-law or single parent family arrangements'. In some countries, controversy instead surrounds the issue of single-sex marriages or civil partnerships where the couple wish to give birth to, or to adopt, children and so create a family unit.

People who seek paternity leave – by which fathers or partners with newly born children may, or may not, be able to take a specified period of time off from work to care for the mother and the family.

POSITIVE DISCRIMINATION, AFFIRMATIVE ACTION, AND QUOTAS

Programmes of *positive discrimination* or *affirmative action*, or *the imposition of quotas*, are used: (i) to deal directly with discrimination in employment or service provision; and (ii) proactively to move an organisation towards the establishment of equality of opportunity. Such programmes are designed to discriminate positively in favour of particular groups, so as:

- To recognise past discrimination and to acknowledge the disadvantage that has resulted from it.

- To equalise the opportunity available to a specified group, so that its opportunity is now equivalent to others against whom there has not in the past been the same level of discrimination.

- To put in place remedial action by which that group may be favoured positively over other groups, thereby raising its status (that is, in terms of its remuneration or its representation in different occupational categories) to an appropriate level of equivalence with other and better represented categories. This might be achieved by the imposition of recruitment quotas or by the establishment of dedicated or group-specific service arrangements.

The use of policies of positive discrimination or affirmative action will require the making of judgements about the definition (and risk) of "under-representation" and the degree of need for remedial action. Programmes of positive discrimination may, for example, be used to increase the proportion of women in decision-making, representational or managerial positions. They may be used where the disabled are deemed to require favoured treatment or where it is thought that there is a need for targeted ethnic-orientated recruitment, for instance, into the uniformed or armed services, social services or teaching. Such targeted (and sometimes quota-based) recruitment is characteristic of the Canadian Federal Government's approach to public sector employment and service provision, and is also found in the United States.

The UK Equality Act 2010, Paragraph 159 makes reference to what it terms "positive action" in the areas of recruitment and promotion.

APPLICATION OF EQUALITY AND DIVERSITY ENACTMENTS

Equality and diversity enactments may apply (*inter alia*) to matters of, or access to, any or all of the following:

- employment, and terms and conditions thereof;

- the provision of goods and services;

- customer service and quality standards;

- public procurement processes and supply chain management;

- proper contractual arrangements or agreements;

- the provision of facilities, premises or places of public access (for example, housing, factories, offices, and institutional construction such as schools or hospitals, shopping or entertainment centres, etc.);

- the provision of transport facilities;

- financial services;

- the provision of occupational pensions;

- educational, medical, uniformed and other public or community/community management services;

- the provision of educational and professional qualifications.

Equality, diversity, opportunity, human rights and discrimination legislation (and where appropriate their related Statutory Codes of Practice in the UK) are applied to the role of individuals, principals, chief executive officers (CEOs), company directors, people responsible for corporate governance, managers, and the staff of organisations who are acting in an agency capacity, whether they be:

- employers;

- the providers of employment-related services;

- public sector buyers responsible for official public procurement processes;

- service providers;

- suppliers of goods and products;

- sub-contractors;

- agents;

- service providers to certain specified professionals (such as the uniformed services; or practitioners of the law, medicine, engineering, accountancy and other chartered or incorporated institutions, etc.);

- trade or membership organisations, trade unions, etc.;

- qualifications or standards bodies;

- a responsible public authority in respect of the "public functions" for whose implementation it is established;

- people responsible for the selection of candidates for public service or political parties.

STANDARD CATEGORIES OF DISCRIMINATION

The second key purpose of any equality and diversity legislation is to ensure that individuals and organisations *do not discriminate*. Proprietors, principals, managers and organisations may not (*inter alia*) cause such discrimination:

- by placing employees, agents or sub-contractors under instruction or pressure to discriminate against others;

- by incorporating discriminatory material into marketing, advertising or selling processes;

- by a failure to incorporate the requirements of prevailing equality enactments into their strategic, governance and operational processes, service provision, performance management and their use of capability or resources, etc.

Four types of discrimination – EU, UK and US legislation typically divide discrimination into the following components:

1. *Direct discrimination* – which is defined to occur when a person is treated less favourably than others in comparable circumstances because of a defined or specified characteristic, such as gender, race or disability, etc.

2. *Indirect discrimination* – which is defined to occur where a "provision, criterion or practice" is applied equally to all but has a differential impact on the members of any particular protected group, of which a complainant is one, so that this group or complainant is placed at a disadvantage as a result.

The EU Council Directive 2000/78/EC describes the relevant provision, criterion or practice as having to be "apparently neutral". It also qualifies the concept of indirect discrimination by suggesting: (i) that the provision, criterion, or practice concerned may be objectively justified by a legitimate aim; and (ii) that the means of achieving that aim may be judged to be "appropriate and necessary", that is, "proportionate".

3. *Harassment* – which is defined as unwanted conduct that violates a person's dignity or exposes them to an intimidatory, hostile, degrading, humiliating or offensive environment on the grounds of a failure or a refusal to accommodate to any of the relevant characteristics, such as race, gender, etc. Harassment is commonly associated with the concept of "bullying". Bullying may be defined as malicious, undermining, humiliating, intimidatory or threatening behaviour aimed at the personal or professional behaviour, or frame of mind of another person. Bullying may demonstrate, or be based on, a misuse or abuse of power or position on the part of the perpetrator. Field states that bullies in the workplace may be 'spiteful, vindictive and destructive and ... use their position of power to practice these traits for their own gratification. In serious cases, bullies may resort to crime' (such as discrimination) in order 'to get rid of or embarrass people into leaving'.

4a *Victimisation* – which is defined as treating a person less favourably because they have taken action in respect of discrimination, for example, by bringing a complaint or giving evidence for a colleague.

4b *Retaliation* – the concept of victimisation is defined in the USA as "retaliation". The US Equal Employment Opportunity Commission comments that 'all of the laws we enforce make it illegal to fire, demote, harass, or otherwise retaliate against people [applicants or employees] because they filed a charge of discrimination, because they complained to their employer [or other covered entity] about discrimination on the job, or because they participated in an employment discrimination proceeding [such as an investigation or lawsuit] ... the law forbids retaliation when it comes to any aspect of employment, including hiring, firing, job assignments, promotions, layoff, training, fringe benefits, and any other term or condition of employment.

OTHER FORMS OF DISCRIMINATION

Other, more extreme forms of discrimination are frequently reported. These include:

• The systematic denial of human rights. For example, Palestinians, whether living in Gaza or as members of the diaspora scattered throughout the Middle East.

• Outright persecution or genocide. For example, black ethnic groups in Rwanda or Southern Sudan in past years.

Such forms of discrimination, however important and unfortunate, have a criminal basis in law. Their analysis is therefore beyond the scope of this book.

INDIVIDUAL AND INSTITUTIONAL SOURCES OF DISCRIMINATION

Discrimination may take place at two levels. The first occurs at *the level of the individual*, whether as principal, employee or service provider. For example, gender-based discrimination against female colleagues is widely reported. It is likely that principals, agents, employers or service providers may be held vicariously liable for such acts. The second occurs at *the level of the institution or corporation*. For example, institutional racism, ageism or homophobia in which discrimination is endemic to the culture and operations of the organisation as a whole. The principals of such organisations, or those held responsible for corporate governance, may be held personally responsible at law for such failures of compliance.

FAILURES OF COMPLIANCE, DISCRIMINATION RISK, AND COST

There are likely to be a variety of risks associated: (i) with an individual or an institutional failure of compliance with EDD law and statute; or (ii) with a breach of the prevailing norms of acceptable or ethical EDD behaviour. These risks may be personal, physical, legal, medical or financial. But in the end they will all take some form of *value loss*. That is, discrimination risk and failures of compliance are almost certainly likely to result in (unplanned or non-budgeted) financial, medicolegal or other kind of *cost*. Such cost may be very substantial, as shown in Chapter 1.

The two main sources of discrimination risk were described immediately above. There may be individual failures of compliance, for which the employer or service provider is likely to be vicariously responsible. There may instead be institutional failures of compliance or duty of care, such as those described by the MacPherson and Bain Reports that dealt with past institutional racism in the UK police, fire and rescue services. These two reports are dealt with in later chapters.

The consequences of discriminatory failures of compliance or duty of care may include any of the following:

- poor employee relations;

- poor customer service and customer relations;

- loss of custom;

- legal fines and costs of lawsuits;

- individual compensation payments, which in the UK might, for example, range from £10,000 to £1 million per person;

- loss of government and public sector contracts. So, for instance, the UK Essex County Fire and Rescue Service states that 'the procurement process is important in ensuring that our policies and practices are not compromised by engaging suppliers that do not reflect our commitment to ... eliminate illegal discrimination. When a contract for goods or services is put out to tender, we will ... require all suppliers to provide us with evidence of their eligibility to be awarded a contract. This includes information on their equal opportunities policies and whether they are or have been subject to formal investigations by any equality body. If a supplier has been found wanting as the result of an investigation, the Service will require evidence that the necessary improvements have been made'. The UK Essex County Fire and Rescue Service goes on to state in respect of sub-contracting that any functions that are contracted out by them 'will undergo an assessment process, particularly where they are in public or highly visible areas. Monitoring processes ... will ensure suppliers and contractors are complying with the undertakings they give when tendering for our contracts';

- poor public relations or actual reputational losses, for instance as described by Garry Honey in a companion volume in this series of Short Guides;

- job evaluation scheme disputes;

- the cost and disturbance of formal enquiries or investigations, whether internal or carried out by external or law enforcement agencies;

- the cost to the taxpayer of formal reports produced by government bodies;

- career damage suffered by responsible staff who have been shown to have failed properly to implement or to enforce the necessary legal, statutory, governance or corporate objectives;

- crises that result from failures of compliance, for instance, as described by Morden (2007). Such crises are dealt with in a later chapter of this Short Guide.

These consequences of failures of compliance or duty of care may also be categorised under *Six Sigma* methodology as "costs of poor quality". The concept of cost of poor quality in an EDD context is described in a later chapter.

In addition, the consequences of failures of compliance may take a personal or physical form. These may include risks of physical or mental health damage to victims of discrimination, such as that suffered by those who have experienced severe work-based stress, burnout and mental breakdown.

In a more extreme case, there are risks of physical injury to those members of the uniformed services who have to confront the consequences of hatred or discrimination in the form of public riots (such as those that have occurred in the UK, France, Italy and the USA), crowd disturbances or incidences of criminal activity that, again, are beyond the scope of this book.

Case example: United States OFCCP settlements from 2007 – on 11 March 2009, the Center for Corporate Equality released a report analysing enforcement results compiled by the US Department of Labor's Office of Federal Contract Compliance Programs (OFCCP) on their equal employment and affirmative actions for 2007. The Report identifies enforcement processes that resulted in the award of $51,680,950 in back pay and annualised salary and benefits for 22,251 American workers who had been subjected to unlawful employment discrimination (source: Internet PD).

UK DISCRIMINATION RISK AND THE STATUTORY ENFORCEMENT OF EQUALITY AND HUMAN RIGHTS

The enforcement by the Commission for Equality and Human Rights (CEHR) of statutory UK equality rights is summarised as follows:

- The CEHR may investigate 'whether or not a person ... has committed an unlawful act' under any of the various equality and human rights enactments.

- The CEHR may issue an 'unlawful act notice' to enforce such compliance as it requires.

- This unlawful act notice may require the preparation of 'an action plan for the purpose of avoiding repetition or continuation of the unlawful act' and 'recommend action to be taken by the person for that purpose'. Compliance means that the person or organisation concerned *must* take action in accordance with this plan or take such specified action as has been required of them.

- Compliance with an unlawful act notice may be enforced at an Employment Tribunal, at a County or Sheriff Court, or ultimately by a process of judicial review.

- A failure to comply without reasonable excuse may represent the committing of an offence (Equality Act 2006, Paragraphs 20 to 22).

In the case of a public sector authority, the CEHR also has the power to issue and to enforce a "compliance notice" requiring response and action where it is not satisfied that the authority is meeting its specific duties of care.

UK Codes of Practice – adherence to any Code of Practice issued by the CEHR (or its predecessors) is required because, while 'a failure to comply with a provision of a code shall not of itself make a person liable to criminal or civil proceedings, but a code:-

a) shall be admissible in evidence in criminal or civil proceedings; and

b) shall be taken into account by a court or a tribunal in any case in which it appears to the court or tribunal to be relevant' (Equality Act 2006, Paragraph 15).

Formal accountability – an individual (such as a chief executive officer or chief constable, etc.), a local government authority or a group of individuals (such as a board of governors or corporate officers) must be identified as the person or persons responsible at law for matters of compliance with the various relevant enactments. This directly affects the process of corporate governance, stewardship and the definition of vicarious responsibility described immediately below.

Employers' and Principals' Vicarious Liability – may be summarised as follows:

- Anything done by a person in the course of his employment shall be treated as being done by the employer as well as by the person.

- Anything done by a person as agent for another shall be treated as being done by the principal as well as by the agent.

- It is immaterial whether an employer or principal knows about or approves of the act.

- But in proceedings against a person in respect of an act alleged to have been done by his employee or agent, it may be a defence for the employer or principal to claim that he took such steps as were reasonably practicable to prevent the employee or agent: (i) from doing the act; or (ii) from doing acts of that kind.

Enforcement by individuals – individuals may seek to enforce their rights through Employment Tribunals or the County Courts in England and Wales, or the Sheriff Courts in Scotland.

POSTSCRIPT

This chapter has analysed key components of the EDD Agenda. It looked at some of the statutory and duty of care responsibilities associated with the implementation and management of that Agenda. It then identified some of the risks and costs of a failure to comply with the requirements of the EDD Agenda.

The Short Guide now proceeds to Chapter 3. That chapter explains some of the basic principles underlying the EDD Agenda. A failure to adhere to those principles in the governance or the management process within an organisation may give rise to significant EDD Risk, irrespective of whether that failure occurs in the employment or the service arena.

③ EDD Principles

Chapter 3 of this Short Guide identifies and explains some of the key principles underlying the formulation and implementation of the EDD Agenda. These principles are listed as follow:

- Human Rights.

- Dignity.

- Justice and Fairness.

- Utility, in which Benefits and Costs are compared.

- Open Systems Theory.

- Genetic Diversity and Requisite Variety.

- Pragmatism in the Implementation of the EDD Agenda.

An understanding of these principles is required for three reasons. The first reason lies in the variety and complexity of the EDD Agenda to which these principles give rise. The second reason lies in the occurrence of EDD Dilemmas that may be caused by the need to apply and to inter-relate these principles in the implementation process. Such Dilemmas may have to be resolved in order to create a viable EDD outcome, and are described in a later chapter. The third reason lies in the degree of EDD Risk associated with any failure to adhere to, or to comply with these principles in the strategic, management, employment or service process.

HUMAN RIGHTS

A *right* means that a person or a group is entitled to something, or is entitled to be treated in a particular way. *Human Rights* include a properly recognised identity and existence, food and shelter, right to work, proper privacy, independence, freedom from arbitrary decision or imprisonment, freedom of choice and freedom of opportunity. Denying those rights, or failing to implement and to protect them, is likely to be considered unprincipled. Human Rights hold that individuals or groups should be treated as valued entities in their own right precisely because they are human beings. Using others for your own purposes is deemed unacceptable if, at the same time, they are denied their own purposes and ambitions.

So, for instance, the UK Commission for Equality and Human Rights (CEHR) is placed under an obligation: (i) to promote awareness, understanding and the protection of human rights; (ii) to promote equality of opportunity; and (iii) to work towards the elimination of unlawful discrimination. More specifically, the CEHR is placed under a duty to work towards the elimination of prejudice against, hatred of, and hostility towards people categorised as protected groups under the Equality Acts 2006 and 2010 as described in Chapter 2. Any

form of prejudice and hostility are directly incompatible with the Human Rights of those people.

DIGNITY

The concept of *dignity* is closely related to that of Human Rights. Dignity is an indicator of how people feel, think and behave in relation to the value that they attribute to themselves, and attribute to others with whom they have dealings. To treat others with dignity is to treat them as being of significant worth and in a manner that respects their value as individuals.

The UK's Royal College of Nursing (RCN) for instance suggests that 'when dignity is present, people feel in control, valued, confident, comfortable and able to make decisions for themselves. When dignity is absent, people feel devalued, lacking control and comfort. They may lack confidence and be unable to make decisions for themselves. They may feel humiliated, embarrassed or ashamed. Dignity applies equally to those who have capacity, and to those who lack it. Everyone has equal worth as a human being'. They should be treated in accordance with their own needs for personal dignity.

The RCN goes on to state of the service environment that 'in care situations, dignity may be promoted or diminished by the physical environment, by organisation culture, by the attitudes and behaviour of the nursing team, and by the way in which care activities are carried out. The nursing team should therefore treat with dignity all people in all settings, and of any health status. This dignified care should continue right up to and beyond the death of a patient' (RCN, 2008).

JUSTICE AND FAIRNESS

Justice and fairness exist when benefits and burdens are distributed equitably and according to an accepted code, rule or policy. The result is conceptualised in terms of "fair shares for all", whether it be of benefits or burdens, or both. If the share of benefits and burdens appear to be fair according to society's rules, then an action will be deemed to be principled.

UTILITY: COMPARING BENEFITS AND COSTS

The concept of utility emphasises the net amount of good that may be produced by a policy, a decision or an action. It uses *utilitarian reasoning*. This is likely to be based on some form of "cost-benefit" analysis, in which the costs and benefits of a policy, a decision or an action are compared. These costs and benefits may be any or all of:

- *economic* (as expressed in measurable values, that is, derived from processes of risk and performance management in an organisation);

- *social* (as measured by indicators of welfare or effect on society);

- *human* (as measured by psychological, emotional or psychiatric impacts).

By comparing the relative costs and benefits of a policy, a decision or an action, the net cost or the net benefit may become apparent. Under this reasoning, if the benefits outweigh the costs, then the action is principled (and vice versa). This notion of utility may be deemed to underpin the concepts of "reasonableness", "reasonable adjustment", "reasonable accommodation", "reasonable treatment", "reasonable practicality" or "degrees of compliance" that appear, for instance, in UK and US legislation associated with Equality, Diversity and Discrimination. The definition of "what is reasonable" is dealt with in a later chapter.

OPEN SYSTEMS THEORY

The UK or US approach to issues of Equality, Diversity and Discrimination Risk would appear to be based on *open systems theory*. Morden (2004) defines a system 'as any entity, whether conceptual or physical, which consists of inter-related, interacting, or interdependent parts. Systems thinkers distinguish between "closed" and "open" systems. Closed systems are self-supporting or self-managing and do not interact with their environment. Open systems do interact with their environment, from which they receive essential inputs such as information and energy. The capacity of an open system to import resources and information from its environment allows it to offset the tendency for all systems to suffer from "entropy", that is, to deteriorate or wear out over time. Organisations [and] social systems are regarded by systems thinkers as open systems ... they must therefore possess the following three characteristics. Firstly, they take in resources and information as inputs from their environment. Secondly, they convert these inputs into an output form, using an appropriate process or technology. Thirdly, they exchange these outputs with their environment, for instance using market or political mechanisms ... it would be inconceivable that the external environment could have no impact on the running of [an] organisation' or a social system.

Thus, the process of implementing and managing the EDD Agenda, for example, in the UK or US may be conceptualised in the terms of an open social system or structure that is characterised by:

- Incoming and up-to-date information flows, whether from individuals, "groups" (and their representatives) or organisations directly affected by the implementation (or non-implementation) of the EDD Agenda, or from legal and academic experts, or from policy-makers, etc.

- Innovative or creative forces driving change in the Agenda that derive from the actions of opinion leaders, interested parties and the media, pressure groups, legislators, charities (such as "Mind"), government campaigns (such as "Time to Change") or simply from individuals who have communicated to the wider world their own experience of discrimination or inequality.

- New external outcomes, whether in the form of legal action or developing case law, emerging compromises and accommodations (such as those associated with military injuries and disability), changing legislation or new codes of practice. Similarly, such developments might take the form of changing attitudes in society or in organisations towards such matters as the promotion of women, the widening of access to the professions or the employment of people from the ethnic minorities, etc.

GENETIC DIVERSITY AND REQUISITE VARIETY

Open systems thinkers believe that in order to offset processes of entropy, corruption or obsolescence, social structures or organisations as social systems must absorb a flow of at least a minimum critical mass of varying or novel external stimuli. This flow is needed in order: (i) to update the information base and processes of the system; and (ii) to ensure its ability to adapt to changing external expectations, innovations and conditions. This flow of external stimuli is defined to have two necessary components, as follow.

Genetic diversity – the first component is that of genetic diversity. Social systems are deemed to require a minimum incoming flow of certain *types* of information and stimuli in order to offset obsolescence or deterioration. In the case of EDD Risk, such types of information or methodologies might include those, for instance, associated with:

- values and competences of strategic, governance and management process;

- customer or client service provision, for instance, in multicultural or polyglot societies, or in societies characterised by an ageing population or increasing mental health issues;

- processes of staff recruitment, training, motivation, compensation, appraisal and development;

- staff and performance management;

- conflict management and resolution;

- organisation structure and culture;

- legal and medical expertise;

- innovation, creativity and new ways of doing things;

- emotional intelligence;

- processes of change management.

These issues are dealt with at various points throughout this Short Guide.

Requisite variety – the second component is that of requisite variety. An open system needs to absorb a minimum level of *variety of information and stimuli within each type or category of genetic diversity* described immediately above. For instance:

- The management of disability risk will have to be based on developing knowledge about: (i) mental as well as physical health issues; and (ii) the medicolegal implications of both types of disability.

- Matters of gender inequality may not easily be separated from issues of equal pay.

- EDD Risk will have to be conceptualised within the context of values and culture, for instance, when dealing with immigrant communities or ethnic minorities.

Case example – The Canadian Financial Post Magazine commented to its readers that as the country's population 'gets more racially diverse, your company had better look a lot more like the market it's trying to sell to. And if you're not drawing from the widest possible labour pool, you're not getting the brightest or the best'.

Some problems of ensuring genetic diversity and requisite diversity – may include situations in which, for example:

- Types and varieties of requisite information or process may be unfamiliar or unpopular, for instance, because: (i) they run counter to the prevailing values, prejudices or installed base of thinking; or (ii) they were 'not invented here'.

- The organisation is characterised by ineffective processes of decision-making in which: (i) the search for decision alternatives is at best based on past or existing precedent; and (ii) there is a high degree of pre-emption (rejection) of any alternatives deemed to be unfamiliar, controversial or threatening to the status quo.

Generic principles and methodologies: (i) of decision-making; and (ii) of concepts of variety, risk, uncertainty, innovation and change are given detailed treatment in the author's texts *Principles of Management* (2e, 2004) and *Principles of Strategic Management* (3e, 2007), both published by Ashgate.

Case study: Getting women on board – the 19–25 November 2009 edition of the UK's *Birmingham Post* led with the front-page headline "Male, Pale and Stale". It declared that 'with so few women in the boardrooms of the West Midlands, is it any wonder that many believe business is failing in the Region?'

The newspaper commented that in analysing the annual reports and website board profiles of the region's leading companies, a recurring theme became apparent. Most board members in the top 50 quoted companies by turnover in the West Midlands are white, in their 50's or 60's and male. Female executive and non-executive board members instead constitute only 6 per cent of the decision-making power of the region's leading firms, placing West Midland women directors in an even bigger minority than at national level where they make up about 12 per cent of FTSE 100 boards. Two out of three of the region's boardrooms are men-only areas.

The newspaper noted that this lack of diversity is raising local concerns that the people at the helm of the region's firms may be increasingly out of touch with the markets they serve and that the quality of decision-making on boards without a broader spectrum of views and experiences may suffer as a result. Its correspondents suggested that:

- The issue of the low proportion of women on the region's boards needed to be addressed in order to allow companies better to reflect the changing nature of the wider economy that they serve.

- Women comprise 50 per cent of the population – if the organisation wants to get the best talent, it has got to be looking at employing and promoting both sexes equally.

- Getting a better mix of experience and skills means that the organisation may achieve a more effective understanding of employees and markets, and better-quality decision-making. If instead the organisation has people with the same life experience and the same point of view, it may come to suffer "group think". This has had significant recent repercussions, for instance, in the retail, advertising and financial services sectors in the UK.

- A study from Catalyst claimed that companies having the highest representation of women in their top management teams financially outperformed companies with the lowest representation of women.

- Company chairmen tend not to know as many women as they do men. When the organisation invites a newcomer to join its board, it has to do so from a position of familiarity and trust. In the past, this has been one of the reasons why the same male faces have appeared on boards in the region.

- Women need to make themselves more visible as they tend not to be as active as men in networking or putting themselves forward, nor may their networks be so deep-rooted.

The newspaper article went on to note that Norway has introduced quotas obliging companies to ensure that 40 per cent of their board members are women, while Sweden and Spain are now also taking a strong approach towards enhanced female representation on company boards.

PRAGMATISM IN THE IMPLEMENTATION OF THE EDD AGENDA

The practical formulation and implementation of the Equality, Diversity and Discrimination Agenda would appear of necessity to have to be based on a significant degree of *pragmatism*. Pragmatism is defined by *Webster's Dictionary* as 'originating in or relying on factual information; relying on experience or observation rather than ... theory; the practice of emphasizing experience, especially of the senses, or relying on sensation rather than intuition, induction or other rationalistic means in the pursuit of knowledge'.

Lessem and Neubauer comment that 'common law based on precedent, behavioural psychology based on directly observable phenomena, and classical science based on visible blocks of matter, all stem from this Anglo-Saxon "feet on the ground" approach'.

A pragmatic approach may also be used to focus on the capacity of individuals, entities and organisations to learn positively on an iterative (repeated) basis: (i) from *precedent* (for example, EDD case law); and (ii) from their *ongoing experience* in order to accumulate and to refine collective wisdom, and to learn from this wisdom in order to develop and progress into the future.

The application of such a pragmatic approach may be illustrated in an EDD context by the long tradition in the travel, tourism and hospitality sectors of employing gay men. An argument may be put forward that the less aggressive and more sensitive characteristics of such men are better suited than heterosexuals to the varying and potentially highly unpredictable patterns of face-to-face customer service in that sector.

Similarly, one large European electro-technical company encourages the recruitment and promotion of women whose husbands or partners work as teachers, nurses or retail staff, etc. Such men will be in a position to take over the domestic and child rearing responsibilities of the household, leaving their partners free to work the necessary long and uncertain hours, to travel away from home and to pursue their careers as the demands of the business require.

POSTSCRIPT

This chapter has described some of the key principles that underlie the formulation and implementation of the EDD Agenda. A failure to understand or to comply with these various principles may give rise to significant EDD Risk.

The Short Guide now moves on to Chapter 4. That chapter looks at the influence of the application of national cultural variables on the formulation and implementation of the EDD Agenda and on the EDD Risk associated with it. Such an internationalised analysis of the subject is necessary because issues of Equality, Diversity, Opportunity and Discrimination are likely to be subject to globalised as well as localised influences.

$\textbf{4}$ EDD Risk and National Culture Variables

This chapter describes the application of national culture variables to the formulation and implementation of the EDD Agenda and to the EDD Risk associated with it. National culture variables are used to construct internationalised or globalised analyses of concepts or phenomena. An internationalised treatment is requisite to the purpose of this Short Guide because issues of Equality, Diversity, Opportunity and Discrimination (and their management) are likely to take both of localised and globalised forms. The chapter makes use of the following national culture variables:

- Trust.

- Individualism.

- Uncertainty Avoidance.

- Masculinity.

- Orthodoxy.

- Communication, Body Language, Personal Space and Proxemics.

An understanding of the relevance to this Guide of these national culture variables is required for at least three reasons. The first reason lies in the added dimensions of the understanding of the EDD Agenda and of EDD Risk to which an internationalised treatment gives rise. A second reason lies in the issue of the very significant need to adapt the nature of employment regimes and service provision in the case of multicultural or polyglot societies, such as the UK, the USA, Canada or France. The third reason lies in the need for international or multinational companies to understand and to manage the varying forms of EDD Agenda and EDD Risk that they face in their different operating locations worldwide.

TRUST

Fukuyama differentiates between "high trust" and "low trust" societies. He notes that societies and organisations characterised by a *low degree of trust* may hold an attitude to risk and uncertainty that takes the form of fencing people in and isolating them with a series of bureaucratic rules. He suggests that advanced industrial societies have created comprehensive legal and contractual frameworks for business organisation, economic transaction, and risk management. Systems of contract and commercial law are in place to ensure the compliance of those with whom people and organisations have to transact affairs. Transactional and behavioural requirements are to a degree pre-specified in codes, such as those associated with the EDD Agenda and laid down by law.

Fukuyama suggests that 'people who do not trust one another will end up co-operating only under a system of formal rules and regulations, which have to be negotiated, agreed to, litigated, and enforced (if necessary by coercive means)'. Fukuyama notes that such rules and laws cost money, without creating the significant positive or added value that may be associated with the *high trust* and professionalised organisation described in a later chapter of this Short Guide. Fukuyama comments that 'legal apparatus, serving as a substitute for trust, entails ... "transaction costs". Widespread distrust in a society ... imposes a kind of tax on all forms of economic activity, a tax that high trust societies do not have to pay'. Such transaction costs, some of which were described in Chapter 1, include:

- organisational and societal mechanisms of supervision and control, for instance as described in terms of McGregor's "Theory X" style of management;

- the need to specify matters contractually, not on a basis of mutual trust;

- the cost of disputes, compensation and payoffs;

- the cost of litigation.

Fukuyama concludes that liberal Anglo-Saxon societies like the UK and the USA now possess 'a tendency towards individualism and a potentially debilitating social atomisation'. He cites the rising use of litigation (such as the so-called "compensation culture") within the business, medical and social environments in these countries as an indicator of the declining level of trust that is associated with increasing individualism, and as evidence of the erosion of the communal values and the social capital that are dependent on trust among colleagues, partners, customers and the wider community.

As a result, the case may be made that policy-makers and legislators have been forced to take a low trust view of their populations generally, and of their employers and decision-makers (whether in the private or the public sector) in particular. This scepticism may, in the case of the UK, have been exacerbated by the traditional lack of equality associated with the UK's social class structure and the centuries of exploitation of working people for which it has been responsible. Other reasons for this low trust view might include:

- cumulating experience and evidence (that is, in case law); associated with

- the continuing reluctance or outright failure of governance bodies, corporations and managers to comply with entirely reasonable and necessary requirements associated with the EDD and opportunity agendas;

- the shortcomings: (i) of strategies of voluntary self-regulation or restraint in the employment arena; or (ii) of policies of so-called "social responsibility";

- pressures from influential opinion formers and opinion leaders who have become adept at using and manipulating the media in order to make their case for change;

- the long and pragmatic tradition of regulation and enforcement by statute, case law and codes of practice aimed at improving the welfare and working conditions of citizens as voters and taxpayers;

- the widespread emergence in organisations of processes of risk and impact assessment described in a later chapter, associated with

- the consequences and costs of failures of compliance (as described in Chapters 1 and 2); and

- the potential consequences and costs of crises deriving from failures of compliance, as described in a later chapter.

INDIVIDUALISM

Hofstede's concept of individualism as a national culture variable may be defined in the context of this chapter as a risk condition where people in work or service environments do not acknowledge or understand, nor want to acknowledge or understand the relevance to them and to the organisation of the Equality, Diversity, Opportunity and Discrimination Agenda. Nor perhaps for the reasons of the strong Anglo-Saxon characteristics of self-opinionation, arrogance, materialism, and personal self-absorption as described by Hofstede and Fukuyama do they care to any great degree about such "inconvenient" matters.

Morden (2004) offers one explanation of this syndrome by noting that in individualistic societies, such as the UK and the USA, 'employer and employees may view their obligations towards each other as instrumental ... and therefore lacking in commitment ... Hofstede suggests that given [an] acceptance of the instrumental nature of [this] employment relationship, the importance of the task or the outcome may take precedence over the character and integrity of [these] relationships'. Issues of opportunity, for example, may be seen by employer or employee as being of secondary significance. The individual can always go off to seek better things elsewhere if he or she chooses, while the employer is perfectly entitled to point this out to any of its "dissatisfied" employees. Opportunity may be conceptualised by the employer only in terms of the strict day-to-day demands and requirements of its mainstream business activity.

On the other hand, where employers have continued to appear apathetic or indifferent to the nature and quality of their relationships with employees, clients or customers, or instead remain indifferent to the wider consequences of these relationships, it is hardly surprising that opinion leaders and legislators have pressed for the external establishment of minimum criteria for what is acceptable employer (and employee) behaviour. The vacuum left by uncaring employers or indifferent employees has been filled since the nineteenth century by a myriad of *ad hoc* and contingency-based legislation that gives protection in a variety of different ways. Legislation associated with the EDD and Opportunity Aagendas simply follow in the footsteps of this reasonable, pragmatic and long-established UK, European and US tradition.

UNCERTAINTY AVOIDANCE

An argument may be put forward that the implementation of the EDD Agenda has in the past been characterised by a lack of priority and by a low degree of acceptance. As a result, policy-makers and legislators seem long ago to have come to the conclusion that the only way to progress matters and to minimise risk in the absence of effective voluntary, self-imposed or "socially responsible" mechanisms is to use the blunt instruments of legislation and enforcement. This is an example of increasing *uncertainty avoidance* and appears to be characterised by:

- An acceptance of the low trust conditions described by Fukuyama.

- A perceived need to fill the vacuum created by the absence of effective voluntary mechanisms, described above, with clear statutory benchmarks for the minimum required forms of opportunity, behaviour and levels of compliance.

- The establishment of extensive formalised and standardised laws, rules, regulations and codes of practice. Morden notes that such formalisation and standardisation is used 'to "cover all eventualities", to "establish policy and contingent decision", or to "eliminate the need to exercise discretion"', thereby reducing the level of risk and uncertainty in the matter to a more acceptable level.

- An increasing reliance on standardised and consistent professional expertise and the use of "expert judgement", for instance as described by the Law Society of Scotland, in the matters of governance, management process, compliance and legal enforcement.

MASCULINITY

Hofstede suggests that the dominant values of a masculine society include assertiveness, aggression and material acquisitiveness. Feminine values, such as co-operation, caring and concern for people, may be considered secondary in terms of leadership, governance and workplace priorities.

Employment and management processes may be seen as masculine activities, irrespective of whether men or women are involved in carrying them out. These processes of employment and management may be seen as having to have a competitive, rational and unemotional character. This may have a number of implications for EDD Risk, for instance, as follow:

- There may now be an acceptance of the philosophy that whilst a duty of care under Health And Safety At Work Act (HASAWA) type legislation is acceptable and necessary, those duties of care associated, for instance, with Equality, Diversity and Opportunity instead represent state interference in the affairs of the organisation. First, the employer should be free to recruit whomsoever it pleases, particularly placing competitive emphasis on candidate merit, competence and excellence of past achievement. Second, if an existing employee does not like his or her lot, then in an open and competitive job market he or she is free to leave to develop their career elsewhere as they like. Career development is ultimately seen in individualistic terms to be the responsibility of the employee, not the employer. Hence, for instance, the legions of full and part-time students pursuing MBA degree courses across the globe.

- There may be an acceptance of a view that in a highly competitive globalised and performance-orientated environment, the concept of the "survival of the fittest" must drive the processes of leadership, governance, employment and management. The weakest may have to "toughen-up", "train up" or go to the wall; or instead seek employment in a more caring (but if necessary less well-paid) environment. Only the "very best" and most "culturally appropriate" people (as defined by the employer) should be recruited for the job, irrespective of whoever and whatever they are. They should then expect to be subjected to the most rigorous and performance-measured work regime (in which work activities are likely to take absolute priority as the person's central life interest) in order to earn their pay and bonuses.

- There may be scepticism about the application to the workplace: (i) of the need for at least a minimum degree of social or interpersonal sensitivity; or (ii) of the concept of "emotional intelligence" whose application is described in a later chapter.

- There may be a covert tolerance at governance or corporate level of aggressive Type "A" behaviour by managers, supervisors or aspiring promotees. While they might have a record as high achievers, Type "A" people may, if they cannot get their own way by more acceptable means, be prone to bullying, to discriminating against others or to denying opportunity to those to whom they have taken a dislike. Similarly, Type "A" people may perceive illness (such as mental illness and depressive conditions) as evidence of weakness in those people who suffer from them. The Type "A" person may well have a view of themselves as being indispensable and indestructible. Like Atlas, it is they who must carry the World on their shoulders. Other people should be like them. If they are not then they must be failures?

ORTHODOXY

Hall differentiates between "high context" and "low context" cultures. Context is defined in this case in terms of how individuals and their society obtain and validate information, develop values and make decisions. People from *high context cultures* will tend to rely on influences from closed personal or family networks. They may mistrust information and opinion from people outside of their circle, group or clan. That is, they may be characterised by the low trust described by Fukuyama in an earlier section of this chapter. Such high context cultures may, over time, become any or all of:

- family, clan or locality dominated;

- inward-looking, "closed" or self-referential;

- traditional or orthodox in mind set, with a strong attachment to past values;

- strongly conventional;

- resistant to change, especially where that change is promoted by "outsiders" who, by definition, are not to be trusted.

Such high context cultures may give rise to EDD Risk in at least two ways. First, they may be resistant to any form of internal change, perhaps refusing to adopt open or more tolerant views of women or "foreigners" in their own scheme of things. Second, they may be reluctant to adopt changing external attitudes, for example, to the role of women, gay persons or representatives of ethnic minorities in the employment arena; or instead find it difficult to meet proper customer service standards when dealing with people whom formally they held in contempt or towards whom they were openly hostile for reasons of religion, social class or caste, or racial background, etc.

Such EDD Risk could then be exacerbated by what may be the typically *low context culture* of EDD policy-makers, legislators or risk managers in advanced industrial or Westernising countries. People from low context cultures will tend to rely on external and objective research or information when making decisions, particularly where this information is evidential and validated. The personal or traditional opinions of others may as a result be viewed with considerable scepticism if they do not conform with what is deemed to be the prevailing, proven, legally and statistically valid "scientific wisdom" in EDD matters. By definition, decisions on the EDD Agenda are likely in such countries to have to be predicated on openness to new evidence and to new ideas. EDD Risk is not static. It is a moving and an adaptive concept, as described in the previous two chapters.

COMMUNICATION, BODY LANGUAGE, PERSONAL SPACE AND PROXEMICS

EDD employment and customer service risk may derive from people who, for whatever reason, hold habitual discriminatory attitudes. Such discriminatory attitudes (for example, as described in Chapter 1) may result: (i) from the masculinity and orthodoxy described in the previous two sections; or (ii) from any form of prejudice, entrenched racism, hostility to women or the disabled, homophobia, etc., that are combined with any or all of the following risk characteristics:

- The use of *explicit forms of communication*, in which people speak as they feel, say exactly what they mean, and to a significant degree are unconcerned with the impact, effect or consequence for other people of what they have said.

- A low or non-existent degree of social or interpersonal sensitivity, or emotional intelligence.

- A negative, contemptuous, or outright hostile use of *body language*, listening behaviour, or personal taste (such as that of deliberately belching or farting, exhaling cigarette smoke, or chewing gum during a conversation).

- The use of inappropriate *personal space* when interacting with others. This may be especially offensive in the case of people of the opposite gender. Physical closeness or touch may appear overfamiliar or threatening when its location occurs inside the reserved space described by the concept of *proxemics* as "intimate".

POSTSCRIPT

This chapter has identified the influence on the EDD Agenda of a variety of national culture variables. A failure properly to understand these variables is likely to give rise to employment and service risks, whether on a local or an international basis.

The next chapter of this Short Guide analyses a series of management or decision-making dilemmas to which the formulation and implementation of the EDD Agenda may give rise. EDD Risk may derive directly from the existence of these dilemmas or instead occur as a result of attempts to resolve them.

⑤ EDD Risk and Management Dilemmas

This chapter identifies Equality, Diversity and Discrimination Risk that derives from *management or decision-making dilemmas* associated with the formulation or implementation of the EDD Agenda. These management dilemmas are listed as follows:

- Opportunity or Excellence?

- Rules or Exceptions?

- What Language?

- Homeland or Multiculturalism?

- The Voice of the Victim.

- What is Reasonable or Proportionate?

The chapter then moves on to suggest ways in which the EDD Risk to which these dilemmas give rise may be defined, understood and where possible resolved.

OPPORTUNITY OR EXCELLENCE?

The EDD Risk inherent in the management or decision-making dilemmas that are the subject of this chapter, may first be illustrated by the issue of reconciling opportunity and excellence. Take, for example, the issue of *access to the professions*. This should be a matter of equal opportunity. The benefits of professional employment may be significant. So may the burdens or costs: (i) of qualifying; (ii) of the performance expectations, risk, difficulty and pressure of the work; (iii) of the likely complexity and the need for personal judgement and discretion; and (iv) of the need for continuing professional development. Access to the professions and the personal benefit this confers should be open to all, not just to a privileged few. On the other hand, all concerned must be prepared to accept the associated costs and burdens, in order that these professions may maintain (and where necessary exceed) the standards of currency and excellence to which they are obliged to operate. Aircraft pilots, for instance, are required to achieve a consistently better than Six Sigma (6σ) success rate of 99.73 per cent in their operations since, by definition, any failure on their part is unacceptable.

Similarly, in commenting on the idea that a political party might as a matter of policy always pick a woman as either its leader or its deputy leader, one UK newspaper editorial gave its opinion that 'only the best should reach the top regardless of gender and untainted by targets or quotas'. Under such a view, the need for individual excellence in leadership and performance is to be placed ahead of concepts of collective good or collective benefit in the relevant scale of priority.

RULES OR EXCEPTIONS?

Risk may stem from the dilemma inherent in any decision about the degree to which the organisation: (i) chooses (or instead perceives that it is required) to adhere strictly to all relevant EDD rules, policies or statutes; or instead (ii) feels it necessary to depart from these rules, policies or statutes when pragmatically it considers such a course of action to be appropriate, proportionate or legal.

The dilemma posed by the existence of rules and the necessity for making exceptions may be illustrated by the use of the quotas associated with programmes of positive discrimination or affirmative action. How rigidly is the organisation obliged to adhere to the rules, for instance, in the matter of recruitment, deployment and promotion? For instance, see the following case study.

Case study: Race, Republicans and Fireman Frank – Patrick Buchanan of *The American Conservative* (Arlington) notes that Frank Ricci 'is a fireman in New Haven, Connecticut, who decided, after 11 years with the department, to pursue his dream of becoming a lieutenant. In order to prepare for the promotion exams, he … spent more than $1,000 buying textbooks and, because he is dyslexic, having them transferred to audiotape. His studying – sometimes 13 hours per day – paid off, winning him one of the eight lieutenant slots open. Alas, none of the eight officers who made the cut were black. So the city, citing an … affirmative action law, disregarded the exam result and promoted no one.

New Haven didn't try to justify its decision on diversity grounds, said George Will in *The Washington Post*. It simply argued that it was protecting itself from being sued. "So, to

avoid defending the defensible in court, it did the indefensible."
The irony is that the city is being sued anyway, by the white
firefighters ...

Ricci was hard done by, said Joan Walsh on *Salon.com*, but ...
the reality is that many of America's fire departments remain
(predominantly) white, and in particular, Irish Catholic. For
years, in San Francisco, the position of fire chief was "handed
down from one Irishman to another, a roster of Sullivans and
Kellys and Murrays and Murphys"; in New York, a city that
is majority black and Latino, the fire department is 91 per
cent white. When I brought this up in a political discussion
on TV, one pundit ... suggested that firefighting was an Irish
Catholic "tradition", much like Italian barbers or Mexican
restauranteurs. But this is a public sector job, not a "family
business". Opening this closed shop up – even with the blunt
tool of affirmative action – is healthy, even if, in Ricci's case,
it has produced an unfortunate result' (source: 'Best of the
American Columnists' – *The Week*, 16th May 2009).

WHAT LANGUAGE?

Language use may present a number of EDD dilemmas, with
their associated risk. These language dilemmas may take one,
or both, of two forms, as follows.

Core language – decisions will have to be made as to what are
the *prevailing core languages* to be used in an organisation or
customer service environment, and who should be speaking
them. For instance, in North America, official use is made
of English, Spanish, French and Innuit, while permutations
of these languages are used as the medium of education,
commerce, healthcare, the public service and government.

Second, decisions will have to be made about the *type of core language* to be used. This might be any of the:

- *standardised*, such as BBC English, official French or standardised (Moscow) Russian;

- *specified or controlled*, relative to personnel specifications, job descriptions and performance expectations, in which any non-fluent or difficult accents are screened out of selection processes for customer service related activities as being inappropriate or unacceptable for operational, safety or quality reasons. Those who fail the necessary testing may have then to be given the opportunity to remedy their communication shortcomings, either at their own expense or at that of the employer, as appropriate;

- *globalised*, such as American English;

- *localised*, in which, for instance, some UK call centres place a customer service emphasis on recruiting people who are deemed to have "friendly" and easily understandable regional accents, such as those of the North East of England, the Central Lowlands of Scotland, and Northern Ireland.

Such choice of language may be justified as being proportionate relative to EDD Risk where it is clearly related to valid and accepted societal norms, or is in advance of those norms, for quality and customer service reasons in an economy, such as the UK, that is predominantly service-oriented.

Third, decisions may have to be made about the actual process of *testing, verifying or certificating language skills*, especially where service type activities are involved. Such testing may take place in the country's educational system, for instance, to indicate exit competence or to permit matriculation. For example, the UK makes use of the General Certificate of School Education (GCSE) and the Advanced (A/S and A) Level systems of exit assessment as validation of language teaching and interim assessment in schools. The US makes use variously of the Language Assessment Scales (LAS), the IPT Language Proficiency Tests, the Woodcock-Muñoz Language Survey (WMLS) and the Language Assessment Battery (LAB) to certify students as English language proficient. Alternatively, testing may take the form of objective "stand-alone" methods such as the:

- International English Language Test (IELTS).

- Test of English as a Foreign Language (TOEFL).

- Graduate Management Admission Test (GMAT).

- Advanced Placement International English Language (APIEL).

The UK General Medical Council requires incoming doctors to take the IELTS test and/or the Professional and Linguistic Training Board (PLAB) Test.

Fourth, some kind of *impact assessment of language decisions* may have to be made, relative to stated task and performance requirements, job descriptions, personnel specifications and training programmes (if any). This impact assessment will have in particular to identify any potentially discriminatory effects on ethnic minorities or immigrants. And where such an impact assessment is made, should it be restricted only to the latter categories or should employers choose (or be required) on grounds of equity to be seen to be testing all applicants or recruits who are to work in what are defined for operational, customer service or safety reasons to be language or communication-sensitive activities, particularly if these activities are categorised (in UK terms) as "skilled" or "highly skilled"? And, again, who should pay for the testing process? The issue of impact assessment is also dealt with in a later chapter.

Quality of language competence – the quality of staff communication skills may be a key variable in the achievement of customer service standards, particularly where for competitive, welfare or political reasons there is a drive towards excellence or Six Sigma outcomes of performance management.

Decisions will therefore have to be made as to what is, or is not, considered to be *an appropriate level or quality of language competence.* Take the case in which an organisation is scrupulously fair in its recruitment, development and promotion policies for all employees. To what extent is it reasonable or legitimate for management to insist on language testing and training for ethnic minority or immigrant staff *only* who may be selected to work in a customer service environment and whose verbal or written communication skills are deemed to be below the minimum specified standard relative to agreed personnel specifications, job descriptions and performance standards for acceptable, safe or successful operations? A minimum level of communication competence may, for instance, be of critical importance in such sectors as medicine, education, transportation, finance, the uniformed services or local government. US law states in this respect that an employer can only require an employee to speak fluent English if this level of language capability is 'necessary to perform the job effectively'. What does "effective" mean pragmatically in terms of customer service and performance management, and who defines it? An "English-only rule", which requires employees to speak English on the job, is only allowed in the US if it is needed to ensure the "safe or efficient" operation of the employer's business and is put in place for non-discriminatory reasons. Again, what do "safe" or "efficient" mean? UK readers may, in this context, bring to mind the controversy over the "parachuting-in" of foreign doctors with poor English language skills to act as temporary night and weekend shift locums in out-of-hours medical practices. In such a case, US law states that an employer may not base a decision to employ a person or to allocate them solely on the basis of the nature of their "foreign accent" unless this accent would seriously interfere with the achievement of the required performance level.

Or instead should *all employees* in such roles be subject without exception to periodic review and testing of their communication capabilities, for instance, by monitoring and reviewing conversations and interactions with customers or clients? And who should pay for this process, at least in the initial stages of appointment to such customer service roles?

HOMELAND OR MULTICULTURALISM?

EDD Risk may on a different level be a function of the degree of compatibility or instead the degree of difference between the *values of the homeland culture* and the *values of multiculturalism or globalisation*. This may have a particular effect on employment and service provision: (i) in multicultural or polyglot societies;

and (ii) where multinational companies and organisations are involved, as described in the previous chapter.

Some homeland cultures, such as those of the UK, Canada and The Netherlands have tended as a result of their past political, imperial and trading histories to develop a relatively multicultural perspective. After all, in the case of the UK, troops guarding Hadrian's Wall that marked a northern outpost of the Roman Empire came from France (Gaul), Spain and Syria. Arab architects and craftsmen were involved in the construction of the great medieval English cathedrals. Black sailors fought for Admiral Lord Nelson at the Battle of Trafalgar and the original trading "taipans" of coastal China were Scots.

Other homeland cultures, such as those of Japan, Korea and Russia tended to be "closed", secretive or conservative. They demonstrate strongly homogeneous and widely shared values and norms that have tended to resist outside influence, particularly that associated with multiculturalism. Foreigners and sailors were even kept in ghettos away from the mass of the populace. Modern global influences on such countries still tend to be consumerist, scientific or materialist, with even these influences adapted to local conditions.

The success of employment and service priorities may depend in such "closed" homelands on how well international operators can realign local mindsets or instead adapt their own policies to local circumstances. This might affect the employment and promotion of women or members of local ethnic minorities, the acceptability of gays and the tolerance of the disabled. Ultimately, the enterprise might have to condition local staff into the acceptance of international standards of customer service by proactive methods of motivation, reinforcement and the visible monitoring of implementation.

Case study: ban the minaret? – the existence of four minarets in Switzerland sparked a national controversy 'which led to a referendum, sponsored by the right-wing populist Swiss People's Party (SVP), proposing a complete ban on the construction of minarets. The government, the other major political parties, and the country's religious and business leaders all campaigned for a "no"; polls suggested that a clear majority opposed the measure. But ... the result was a "shocking success" for the far Right. 57.5 per cent of the electorate, and 22 of the 26 cantons, voted in favour of the ban. It was a triumph for "fear and ignorance", said François Modoux in *Le Temps* (Geneva) – an attack on religious freedom, and a "resounding slap in the face" to Muslims ... Switzerland's 400,000 strong Muslim minority – mostly made up of Bosnians, Albanians and Turks – is well integrated and moderate: you seldom see the veil ... in Swiss streets. Yet the SVP's alarmist campaign managed to exploit lurid fears about fundamentalist Islam ... the party's posters showed minarets rising like missiles from the Swiss flag, next to a fully veiled woman. It is a testament to the "absurd power of prejudice" said Laurent Joffrin in *Libération* (Paris) that the cantons with the fewest Muslims were most solidly in the "yes" camp. The cities, where the Muslims actually live, voted strongly against the measure'.

The consequences of the vote might prove significant, according to *Le Matin* (Lausanne) which stated that 'the vote has done "spectacular" damage to Switzerland's image – of neutrality, and respect of human rights rooted in its long tradition of religious tolerance. The country's luxury brands rely heavily on Muslim nations, and there are fears that Arab wealth could be withdrawn from the country's banks' (source: 'Switzerland's "slap in the face" to Muslims' – *The Week*, 5 December 2009).

Case study: gay bishops – a gay woman priest has been elected as the Suffragan Bishop of Los Angeles. *The Week* commented that 'if her election is confirmed by the Episcopal Church – as looks likely – Canon Mary Glasspool will be the second openly gay bishop in the global Anglican Fellowship. The Archbishop of Canterbury, Rowan Williams, said the election raised "serious questions" about the future of the Anglican communion and the place of the American church in it. He had previously urged a moratorium on gay bishops and same-sex blessings to ease tensions within the church' (source: 'The World at a Glance' – *The Week*, 12 December 2009).

THE VOICE OF THE VICTIM

Chapter 2 summarised the different groups or categories that are typically subject to legislation for Equality, Opportunity, Diversity and Discrimination. Each of these groups has some kind of "voice" in the employment and service arenas. Such voices may, however, vary in strength and influence at different times and under different circumstances.

Some, like the collective voices of professional women or certain ethnic minorities (such as the British Army's fearsome and invaluable Gurkha troops) may be heard loudly and clearly in the promotion of their demands. Such a volume of the voice of the victim was also heard in the case of the London murder of the black teenager, Stephen Lawrence. The resulting MacPherson Enquiry is dealt with in its EDD context in the next chapter.

Other voices, like those of the mentally ill or the unmarried daughters of the orthodox (described in Chapter 4), or some

First Nations People in North America may instead only be heard with difficulty, if at all.

This raises the dilemma of how to recognise and deal with the voices of victims amid the welter of information flows and messages competing for attention that characterise a busy organisation. What can you hear and to what do you pay attention? The resolution of this dilemma posed by the uncertain voice of the victim may depend on three variables, as follow.

The first is the *visibility* of the victim. How visible are his or her concerns and the risks associated with them? A person in a wheelchair is easily seen. Someone with mental health problems may instead appear perfectly normal for most of the time, whether at work or as a client. They will not be wearing a bandage around their head but may still be disabled! Ultimately, to Western eyes, an Asian woman wearing a burka may not be deemed to be visible at all? Is she not an individual with the same entitlements and opportunities as anyone else? Or, as in the French and Belgian view, is she instead the de-personalised and subservient chattel of her husband and his family, forever deprived of her secular and human rights?

The second variable is the *threshold* at which others take notice of the victim. This, again, may vary from place to place. Groups who suffer from low status or minimal influence (such as asylum seekers in the UK or the children of marginalised immigrants) may find it hard to obtain recognition or resolution of the discrimination they suffer. It may take catastrophic events, whether at home or abroad, to take individuals from such groups to a point at which notice is taken of their suffering. Indeed, such events as child homicide; forced marriage and so-called "honour killings"; deaths, injuries or illnesses suffered in the course of illegal employment or exploitation; or squalid living conditions may only end up being dealt with when they have reached a threshold of criminal status.

The third variable is that of the potential for the use of *countervailing force*, by which (whether actively or by default) there is: (i) resistance to hearing the voice of the victim; or (ii) a deliberate downgrading of its importance. Such countervailing force may, for example, be based on negative attitudes or prejudice that result from entrenched or conventional values and predispositions that are hostile towards some or all of the EDD Agenda. The concept of such countervailing force is dealt with in more detail in Chapter 7.

WHAT IS REASONABLE OR PROPORTIONATE?

Newspaper editorials commented, at the time of writing, about the ongoing dilemma faced by the UK government in promoting fairness and equality. On the one hand, there must be an EDD Agenda based on the protection of human rights and the promotion of justice, opportunity and fairness, as described in Chapter 3. On the other hand, there will have to be a *reasonable implementation strategy* available. This could be based: (i) on a comparison of the relevant costs and benefits of the EDD Agenda in which; (ii) a pragmatic (or instead a "business-friendly"?) view is taken at any particular time of the utility to be obtained from policies associated with equality and diversity. In such a case, and in order to calculate any order of short-term priority, the incidence: (i) of economic and financial cost or disturbance and the demands of performance management in an organisation may have to be weighed; (ii) against the social and human benefits to be gained.

Thus, for instance, a college or university may have to make judgements in respect of disability legislation about the level of investment it must make in upgrading its buildings and facilities to an appropriate level of "wheelchair friendliness" without at the same time knowing in advance how many physically handicapped students it will actually recruit each year. So, it might reasonably choose to prioritise its expenditures on a cost-benefit basis, concentrating wheelchair access and safety investments in teaching buildings, Information Technology resources, libraries, pathways and student facilities. It would then provide disability-trained staff to take students in wheelchairs to other locations, such as laboratories, which they are less likely to have a frequent need to visit or require to visit only on specific or timetabled occasions.

The process of the management of the Equality, Diversity and Discrimination Agenda might therefore have to be informed by the *pragmatic and cost-beneficial* view, described in Chapter 3, of what is considered to be "reasonable" or "proportionate" in political, organisational or resource terms and in time scales. For instance, there may be a need to streamline, to optimise or to simplify the processes of action, monitoring, reporting and review in order to avoid creating an excessive bureaucracy that may create negative organisational perceptions of the opportunity agenda. Advice to UK schools, for example, suggests steps that may be taken by educational institutions in order 'to *minimise the additional work required* to demonstrate they are meeting their legal obligations in respect of equal opportunities ... there is a duty to assess and to monitor the impact of policies on pupils, staff and parents, in particular the attainment levels of pupils from different racial groups. Such steps as are *reasonably practicable* should be taken to publish annually the results of the monitoring'. Another way of achieving this lies in the creation of "Single Equality

Schemes". Advice to UK schools suggests that in order to minimise the burden created by the need to comply with the various statutory duties 'we recommend that schools produce a single equality plan' covering all of the stated requirements. Single equality schemes are also proposed by the Law Society of Scotland, the Essex County Fire and Rescue Service, and by the Cleveland Police. Such co-ordinated schemes are at this time of writing the subject of legislation associated with the UK Equality Act 2010.

Resource allocation – the process of the management of the Equality, Diversity and Discrimination Agenda is also likely to be described in terms of the *absolute and relative level of resources available*. The larger the organisation or the greater the level of resources and capability deemed to be available to it, the lower will be the threshold at which a full and comprehensive level of compliance will be required and the greater will be the expectations of its performance. Certainly, public sector organisations are likely to be expected to demonstrate consistent levels of the achievement of excellence or best practice.

This argument is, however, complicated by the issue of "fair shares for all". Not everyone works for large and well-funded organisations. Nor is everybody aware of their rights and entitlements under the law, nor are they necessarily able to fight for them.

Ultimately, therefore, the decision as to what is a reasonable level of resource allocation to the Diversity Agenda within the organisation or the service environment may be taken *by default*. This means the interpretation by lawyers of the relevance of case law and legal precedent to the situation at hand. The outcome of such a form of external enforcement may then be complicated by issues of status and bargaining power, by the behaviour of Employment Tribunals and law courts, and by the values and objectives of the legal profession.

Making reasonable adjustment – the concept of reasonable adjustment is associated with disability discrimination. Both of UK and US law require an employer to provide some kind of *reasonable adjustment* or *reasonable accommodation* for applicants and employees with a disability. The US Equal Employment Opportunity Commission defines reasonable accommodation as any change in the work environment (or in the way in which things are usually done) to help a person with a disability to apply for a job, to perform the duties of a job or to enjoy the benefits of employment. The UK Disability Discrimination Act (DDA) 1995 notes in respect of employment (Part II Section 6 Paragraphs 1 to 3) 'that:

1. Where (a) any arrangements made by or on behalf of an employer; or (b) any physical features of premises occupied by the employer place the disabled person concerned at a substantial disadvantage in comparison with persons who are not disabled, it is the duty of the employer to take such steps as it is reasonable, in all the circumstances of the case, for him to have to take in order to prevent the arrangements or feature having that effect.

2. Subsection (1) above applies only in relation to: (a) arrangements for determining to whom employment should be offered; and (b) any term, condition or arrangements on which employment, promotion, a transfer, training or any other benefit is offered or afforded.

3. The following are examples of steps which an employer may have to take in relation to a disabled person in order to comply with subsection (1) above:

   a) making adjustments to premises;
   b) allocating some of the disabled person's duties to another person;
   c) transferring him to fill an existing vacancy;
   d) altering his working hours;
   e) assigning him to a different place of work;
   f) allowing him to be absent during working hours for rehabilitation, assessment or treatment; giving him ... training;
   g) acquiring or modifying equipment;
   h) modifying instructions or reference manuals;
   i) modifying procedures for testing or assessment;
   j) providing supervision;
   k) providing a reader or interpreter'.

What is considered to be a reasonable form of adjustment in the UK may also be a function of statutory regulation, case law or Code of Practice. At the time of this writing, the relevant Code of Practice may only be enforced in the UK public sector.

Alternatively, decision-makers will have to make their own judgement as to what would be considered reasonable or proportionate under the particular circumstances, for instance in the potentially difficult (and possibly contentious) issue of the management of mental health disability, knowing that whatever judgement is made in the UK could be tested at Employment Tribunal and, if found wanting, a different resolution enforced by due legal process. This is because the onus may be placed on the employer or service provider to show that their actions were reasonable or were instead a proportionate means to achieving an objective and legitimate aim. In the US, a reasonable accommodation is required unless its provision would cause significant difficulty or expense for the employer. Such "undue hardship" is defined to mean that the reasonable accommodation would be too difficult or too expensive to provide: (i) in the light of the size and financial resources of the business; or (ii) in terms of its operational needs. Similarly, the UK Disability Discrimination Act (DDA) 1995 notes (Part II Section 6 Paragraph 4) that in determining whether it is reasonable for an employer to have to take a particular step in order to comply with its obligation to make reasonable adjustment, regard shall in particular be had to:

a) the extent to which taking the step would prevent the effect in question;
b) the extent to which it is practicable for the employer to take the step;
c) the financial and other costs which would be incurred by the employer in taking the step and the extent to which taking it would disrupt any of his activities;
d) the extent of the employer's financial and other resources;
e) the availability to the employer of financial or other assistance with respect to taking the step.

The Equality Act 2010 strengthens UK legislation by requiring the employer to demonstrate that its actions are, in some kind of objective sense, motivated by the need to achieve a legitimate aim or purpose associated with the management or operations of the organisation.

DILEMMAS, EDD RISK AND RESOLUTION

This chapter has suggested some dilemmas associated with the formulation and implementation of the EDD Agenda. Such dilemmas are likely to give rise to a variety of forms of EDD Risk, which may be identified and managed as follow.

Defining and resolving dilemmas – the degree of EDD Risk may in part be a function of the degree to which any particular dilemma can be defined, understood and resolved. There could be four components of such a process.

The first component lies in the "location" of the two outer or extreme ends of the continuum that defines the parameters of the dilemma in question. For example, identifying what are "totally reasonable" and "totally unreasonable" outcomes; "efficient" or "inefficient" outcomes; outcomes that meet or do not meet required quality expectations (that is, as defined by the Six Sigma, Best Value or excellence methodologies to which reference is made at various points in this Short Guide); or primarily homeland-oriented and primarily globally-oriented outcomes.

The second component lies in agreeing what outcomes lie between these two extreme ends of the dilemma. For example, reasonable, efficient or cost-beneficial degrees of compliance; acceptable customer service outcomes; or the reaching of sensible local/global accommodations or compromises.

The third component lies in the available level of resource or capability, to which the potential for the resolution of EDD dilemmas may be directly proportionate. The: (i) more substantial the available resource; (ii) the stronger the capability to hand; or (iii) the more extensive the necessary relationship architecture, the better or more robust may be the resolution.

The fourth component lies in establishing the degree to which there is in principle or in practice likely to be an acceptable resolution to any particular dilemma. For example, inflexible laws enshrining positive discrimination that are insensitive to contingent circumstances, such as those described in the case study 'Race, Republicans and Fireman Frank', above; or the appointment of females to direct combat or weapon systems roles in the armed forces, such in the infantry or air attack; or the impact of entrenched caste systems. A difficulty with the implementation of the EDD Agenda in such cases is that there may always be an outcome that is unsatisfactory or unacceptable to someone or other.

Statute and case law – risk may arise from the definition by statute or case law of the EDD Agenda. This definition may be a function of any or all of:

- the values and attitudes of legislators;

- the values, attitudes, and motivation of lawyers and the legal profession;

- any cultural desire for conflict, condemnation and punishment rather than accommodation, resolution or compromise. This may be associated with

- the developing syndrome of suing for large sums of money as recompense (the so-called "compensation culture").

Under this logic, the process of implementing the EDD Agenda in the fields of employment and customer service itself becomes a key source of risk, for which there may be little or no assistance from legislators and the creators of case law, who may of necessity have different agendas from employers, service providers or customers.

The voice of the customer – methodologies are used in the Six Sigma process to specify the most critical requirements of the client or customer, the parameters and constraints of which are then used to shape the necessary outcomes or outputs of service provision.

The quality or fitness for purpose of these outputs may be defined in terms of customer service by the formula $Q \times A = E$ where:

the quality of the solution (Q) × the acceptability of that solution (A) = the effectiveness of that solution (E).

The achievement of optimal customer service at the level of quality of 4σ (95.46 per cent) or 6σ (99.73 per cent) may therefore have to be balanced against any EDD Risks associated with achieving such an outcome. For example, the quality of cleaning by poorly paid multiracial or immigrant staff of hospital wards and the resultant freedom (or otherwise) from serious patient infection. At the time of writing, this Cost Of Poor Quality issue remains controversial in the UK's National Health Service (NHS), particularly where for cultural reasons the customer service priorities of NHS managers and staff remain low.

The issue of performance management is dealt with in Chapter 6.

Event characteristics and EDD implementation uncertainties – the degree of EDD Risk posed by any of the dilemmas described in this chapter may be defined by the nature of their event characteristics. These could, for example, include any of:

- *Ambiguity of perception, interpretation or meaning.* This may render the identification of any resolution problematic or uncertain. For example, situations in which employment and customer service requirements collide, as in the case of the language issue already described above.

- Significant *change in EDD meaning,* which will require new attitudes or different thinking about the dilemma or its resolution. For example, the rapidly rising risk and cost of stress-based mental health illness now affecting professional and executive staff in the developed economies, as compared with the more familiar physical disability.

- An EDD Agenda whose *varied or complex nature* increases risk and renders resolution more difficult. For example, the variety and complexity of polyglot multicultural societies as found in the UK, the USA, Canada and France.

- An EDD context which is *internally inconsistent.* For example, look: (i) at the myriad legislation dealing with EDD issues in the UK or the USA; (ii) at the different types, levels and pragmatism of employment and customer service resolution they require; and (iii) the problem of creating the harmonised Single Equality Schemes described in an earlier section of this chapter.

- A *novelty or infrequency of occurrence or experience.* The more an EDD event or issue arises, the more familiar people will become with it, and the easier may become its resolution. Conversely, the more unfamiliar or unusual the issue or event, the more problematic may its resolution be. One example is the creation of law and enforcement agencies based on the employment and training of First Nation peoples, which has initially proven difficult in Canada. Another example is the case of forced marriage (with its potential for "honour killings") in the UK and Pakistan whose organisation was (and remains) kept well "below the radar" by its perpetrators. These people are well aware that local UK schools who notice the occasional, unexplained and permanent disappearance of young British-born female students may not be in any position to do much about the matter apart from reporting it to the Police.

- *Value or values implication,* in which, for example, the values of employee opportunity and performance excellence come into direct conflict, as illustrated in earlier sections of this chapter.

- *Cultural or cross-cultural implication,* by which, for example: (i) customer service variables remain unaligned for cultural reasons, as in the case of conflicting attitudes towards the validity of language capability and language testing described in an earlier section of this chapter; or (ii) where the appointment or promotion of women to high value customer or client service roles within multinational companies operating in countries characterised by a significant degree of masculinity or orthodoxy are likely to require executive policy decisions by boards of directors.

- An *unpredictable or varying facility for practical implementation,* perhaps caused by the incidence of any of the event characteristics being described in this section; or arising instead from a failure by legislators, policy-makers or those responsible for corporate governance clearly to specify the means or the methodologies by which desired EDD outcomes are to be achieved.

The generic concepts of event characteristics and decision-making are described in Chapter 9 of the author's *Principles of Management* 2e (2004).

Defining what is reasonable or proportionate – in summary, this chapter has suggested that what is defined to be reasonable or proportionate might be a function of:

- the practicalities of implementation;

- the opportunity or the ability to resolve dilemmas;

- what is defined to be reasonable or cost-beneficial in circumstances of resource constraint;

- the absolute and relative levels of capability and resource available;

- what is defined in implementation terms (if any) by statute or case law, by judgements (if any) as to what constitute proportionate means of achieving objective and legitimate aims, or by Codes of Practice where these are available;

- the principle of fair shares for all.

POSTSCRIPT

This chapter has described a variety of EDD Risks deriving from management or decision-making dilemmas associated with the formulation and implementation of the EDD Agenda. The chapter has suggested ways in which such risk dilemmas may be defined and understood, and where possible resolved.

The Short Guide now moves on to the first of its three final chapters. The purpose of these three chapters is to deal with practical issues of implementing the EDD Agenda including performance management, change management and the strategic management of EDD Risk.

(6) EDD Risk, Leadership and Performance Management

This chapter looks at the leadership and performance management of the EDD Agenda. The objective of the chapter is to identify some of the practical "what to do" and "how to do" elements of the management of that agenda. The chapter describes a straightforward *path* or *pathway* to achieving the necessary EDD performance outcomes and to minimising the EDD Risk associated with the implementation process. The chapter is based on the analysis and inter-relationship of a series of key variables. These variables are:

- EDD Context.

- Tasks.

- Managing Relationships.

- Roles, Responsibilities, Leadership and Accountability.

- Attitudes and Values.

- Emotional Intelligence and Professional Competence.

- Managing Performance and Achieving Results.

These variables are derived from an objective, transactional and process-oriented approach to the leadership and performance management of the EDD Agenda.

EDD CONTEXT: IDENTIFYING THE EQUALITY, DIVERSITY AND DISCRIMINATION AGENDA

The first five chapters of this Guide have identified some of the key features of the Equality, Opportunity, Diversity and Discrimination Agenda, and have described some of the EDD Risks associated with it. This is *the EDD context*. The governance and management of the organisation will have to analyse and to understand the implications of this EDD context. It will then have to communicate this understanding within the organisation and externally to its stakeholders, partners, suppliers and agents. This will imply two practical steps, as follow.

The organisation will, first, have to carry out an evaluation of the degree to which Equality, Diversity, Opportunity and Discrimination characterises its operations and those of its stakeholders, agents or partners. This is likely to require the establishment of an appropriate and accurate base of group information categorising gender, ethnicity, religion or belief, age, etc. This information base will be used to underpin decision-making about employment, training, service provision and so on.

There will, second, have to be a definition of the actual or potential sources of discrimination within the organisation and its external relationship architecture. There will be a need for an objective understanding of what kinds of discrimination have been reported and why that discrimination has occurred. The preparation of such an analysis may potentially be a highly sensitive process. This will require a committed level of championing and a proactive degree of leadership at the governance and strategic management levels. Issues of leadership, championing and governance are dealt with in later sections of this chapter.

TASKS: IDENTIFYING WHAT HAS TO BE DONE AND WHAT ARE THE CAPABILITIES REQUIRED TO DO IT

The implementation of the EDD Agenda and the management of the risks associated with it will give rise to a variety of *tasks*, and to the need to ensure that *capabilities* appropriate to their implementation are in place. These include any or all of the following.

Some core tasks – there will be a requirement to define and agree the needs, obligations and priorities of the Equality, Diversity, Opportunity and Discrimination Agenda. The Law Society of Scotland (LSS), for instance, suggests that *core features* of the process of managing equality and diversity include the following:

- being able (and willing) to recognise and to understand difference;

- placing emphasis on the benefits of equality and diversity;

- prioritising the equality and diversity agenda;

- linking equality and diversity to organisational and business or service objectives;

- understanding EDD Risk issues;

- ensuring compliance with legislation, case law and codes of practice, whether through motivation, encouragement or direct enforcement.

Some strategies by which to implement the EDD Agenda – there will be a need to establish strategies by which to *implement* the Equality, Diversity, Opportunity and Discrimination agenda. These strategies might, for example, be communicated in the form of published equality or diversity "schemes" required by statutory public sector codes of practice in the UK, or instead take the form of a comprehensive "single equality scheme", such as that of the Law Society of Scotland, or that likely to be required by UK law.

Morden (2004) suggests that these strategies might address any or all of the following, as described below.

Human resource planning, for instance, remedying actual or perceived "imbalances" in employment categories, such as the number of women in operational or management positions or the proportion of ethnic minorities employed.

The formulation of performance – related job descriptions and personnel specifications, for instance, on a basis of capability or competence, such that potential discriminatory features are eliminated at source.

The recruitment and selection process, such that all types of applicants are sought and selected within the spirit and requirements of the prevailing laws, codes of practice and company statements of purpose (such as a commitment to act as an equal opportunity employer). The Law Society of Scotland, for example, has proposed competence-based recruitment based on "neutral" principles in which limits are placed on the use of personal identifying data in the selection process and a degree of objective testing of candidates is outsourced, for instance, to a sector-specific body established for that purpose.

Training and development processes associated with the building and reinforcement of the required capabilities. There will be a need to provide the staff and agents of the organisation with appropriate knowledge, skills and motivation relevant to the implementation of the Equality and Diversity Agenda, and relevant to the avoidance of discrimination. This process of training and development will have to include staff involved at the governance level who hold legal responsibilities as principals.

Staff performance appraisal, such that the staff evaluation process used by the organisation is relevant, objective and neutral. The risk that performance criteria may not be applied equally and without favour to all may imply that the staff appraisal system could constitute a source of unlawful discrimination and whose administration may then have to be subject to the process of "impact assessment" described in Chapter 8. The "robustness" and objectivity of the staff appraisal process, relative to the required staff performance capabilities, competencies and outcomes, may be an indicator of enterprise commitment to the equality and diversity agenda, and to making it work in a manner that is conspicuously fair to the majority as well as the minority.

Promotion, such that no eligible person is excluded from consideration on "non-relevant" (that is, discriminatory) grounds and that the criteria for success are objective and clearly understood, and properly applied by all concerned.

Remuneration systems, such that payment and reward are based on objective or competency criteria and not on discriminatory grounds, such as gender or race. This is, at the time of writing, a major issue in the UK where there are significant differences between the private sector pay of men and women, and between local and immigrant labour. Issues of equal pay were described in Chapter 2.

Management capability issues – there will in particular be a requirement to define the consequences for *line or departmental management capability* to deal with operations, staff and risk associated with the EDD Agenda. The need to be seen to optimise opportunity and to eliminate the risk of discrimination may have a number of implications for the tasks, responsibilities and required capabilities of line managers. These may include:

- The shaping at governance and strategic management levels in the organisation of detailed policies for management action and risk assessment.

- The training of line managers in diversity management and in the nature and consequences for the organisation of discriminatory behaviour in employment and service provision.

- The clarification of the locus and nature of the supervision of line management actions, whether at corporate level or by using functional specialists who are allocated the authority to ensure a consistent level of compliance from operational managers.

Compliance issues – there will also be a need to establish consistent policies and capability by which to deal with any incidence of non-compliance, discriminatory behaviour, harassment and bullying associated with the Equality, Diversity, Opportunity and Discrimination Agenda. The complaints, grievance, disciplinary and dismissal processes in use in the enterprise will have to be adjusted to the requirements of such policies and will need to be reinforced through appropriate forms of communication, training and motivation. The Essex County Fire and Rescue Service (ECFRS) notes in this context that it 'recognises the importance of training staff in relation to our duties ... and ensuring staff have the skills and understanding to challenge inappropriate behaviour and help to eliminate ... unlawful discrimination'.

MANAGING RELATIONSHIPS

The implementation, performance management or enforcement of the agenda for Equality, Diversity, Opportunity and Discrimination takes place within the internal and external relationships or architecture in which the organisation is involved. Two key issues under this heading are described below.

Relationships, communication and engagement – the management of equality and anti-discriminatory processes will have to be framed within appropriate forms: (i) of communication and consultation with; or (ii) the involvement of staff, clients or customers and with relevant external groups, agents and partners. For example, the ECFRS gives the example of under-represented, minority, "hard to reach", refugee and asylum-seeker groups that may be on the margins of community safety service provision. The LSS notes of the UK legislation that 'the Race and Gender Equality Duties use the term "consultation" whilst the Disability Equality Duty uses the term "involvement", seen by many as a higher standard which goes beyond gaining feedback through consultations to actual participation in processes. The Society's policy ... took account of this debate and best-practice ... and set the "involvement" standard as the one that we would apply to all strands of our equality work, even prior to this becoming a legal requirement in relation to disability'. Appropriate communication processes may include:

- verbal and written explanation or translation;

- interpretation services;

- the use of simplification processes (for example, at the level of concepts, perceptions or semantics);

- the use of large print, Braille, audio reproduction, signing for the deaf, etc.;

- the use of cultural or cross-cultural awareness and training;

- the development of appropriate change management competencies, as described in Chapter 7.

The effectiveness of this communication process is likely to need to be monitored in order to identify the existence of any information barriers or filtering and to ensure that appropriate types and levels of feedback are being received. There will be a need for such mechanisms of feedback in order that the organisation may monitor, control, review or scrutinise processes of equality and diversity management so as: (i) to achieve the required performance outcomes; and (ii) to demonstrate cumulative improvement. In the UK public sector, processes of monitoring, review and action in respect of the statutory equality categories are subject to audit and to annual public report. For instance, the ECFRS states that elements of its Equality Scheme are audited as a part of the process of annual internal audit by Price Waterhouse Cooper, using Best Value Performance Indicators (BVPIs).

External architecture, partners and stakeholders – it may be the case, as in the UK and the US, that the accountability of the organisation for its statutory and regulatory obligations for Equality, Diversity, Opportunity and Discrimination will also apply to some degree to its external architecture of suppliers, partners, agents and stakeholders. The ECFRS, for example, notes that the partnerships in which it participates vary in size and remit, and may be formed as a result of statutory requirement or instead to meet the specific needs of the community. The partnerships as architecture may not necessarily in themselves be bound by the General UK Duty to avoid unlawful discrimination and their members may be legally responsible for their own decisions and actions. However, the ECFRS states that 'as a Fire Authority we have a responsibility to ensure that the partnerships (in which it is involved) take account of the General Duty ... and that all members of the partnership are aware of our commitments and responsibilities'. This, for example, applies to the processes of sub-contracting or purchasing and supply, described in Chapter 2.

ROLES, RESPONSIBILITIES, LEADERSHIP AND ACCOUNTABILITY

The Law Society of Scotland is, for instance, of the view that four factors influence the successful development and implementation of equality and diversity policies. These factors are listed as follows:

- clear statements of role and responsibility;

- leadership and accountability;

- prioritising or "mainstreaming" the duty into core functions;

- the proper training of staff and the development of capability and expertise. This factor has already been described in an earlier section of this chapter.

The first three of these factors are used to structure the content of this section of Chapter 6 on roles and responsibilities.

Roles, responsibilities and accountability: from governance to executive action – organisations will have to use appropriate concepts of accountability exactly to define what are the responsibilities of those people charged with corporate governance and what are to be the strategic and operational responsibilities of boards, elected officials, governors and executive staff in the implementation of the Equality, Diversity, Opportunity and Discrimination Agenda. For instance, the ECFRS notes that 'functions, including commands are ... responsible for integrating equality plans and equality targets into their annual business, safety and risk profile plans. These are reported and reviewed annually through the business planning process'. A proper understanding of the legal relevance of the concepts of "principal" and "agent", and of their responsibilities as described in Chapter 2, will be essential in this context.

Leadership and championing – traditional approaches to the management of equality and diversity are described by the LSS. It suggests that organisations have 'tended to take a compliance-driven, reactionary and/or tokenistic approach to the subject meaning that the term has often been relegated to little more than a cliché. Human Resource/Personnel departments were traditionally responsible for implementing Equal Opportunities Strategies and even where this was done to a high standard there was often a failure to transfer the skills and best practice to other business areas, [for instance] in relation to [employment and] service delivery'.

The current received wisdom is instead that there will be a need for effective leadership at the governance and strategic levels to drive the establishment, implementation, monitoring and review of equality and diversity processes. That is, there is a need for equality and diversity champions who are appointed at governance, corporate or senior levels: (i) to drive the necessary agenda forward; and (ii) to ensure the motivation and compliance of people in the organisation and its agents.

So, for instance, the Essex County Fire and Rescue Service Equality Scheme 2006–2009 sets out the Chief Fire Officer's personal commitment as Chief Executive Officer to achieving equality and respect for diversity throughout the Service. As ECFRS Diversity Champion, he states that he is 'committed to ensuring that we promote equality and diversity in all our employment policies, and [in the] services [that] we deliver to the communities within Essex'.

The Chief Constable of Cleveland Police notes in his force's Equality Scheme 2007–2010 that 'as both service provider and employer, Cleveland Police has a legal and moral duty to promote equality and tackle discrimination. I am therefore committed to ensuring that members of the force play their part in helping to eliminate discrimination and promote equality, so that we provide a policing service and working environment that is appropriate and welcoming ... through the application of this scheme we are moving the subject of Diversity away from the "bolt-on" position that it occupied in the past and making it a core consideration in everything we do. Changes in policing have led to a greater transparency in decision-making, an increase in the levels of accountability and a growth in community involvement. Such change brings with it an increased exposure of our working practices and therefore a greater potential for criticism. Although this may prove uncomfortable at times it is through such exposure and consultation that we will ensure that the policing we deliver is in keeping with the needs of a diverse and changing community. Through strong leadership, a proportionate approach, effective partnerships, and a supportive workplace we will continue to deliver the message that Cleveland Police values diversity and that discrimination will not be tolerated'. The Deputy Chief Constable, as Cleveland Police Force Diversity Champion, goes on to reinforce the view that 'diversity and inclusion must be core values ... if we are to provide secure neighbourhoods and communities ... it is vital that no individual is treated less favourably than any other, and that each member of our community receives a service from Cleveland Police that is appropriate to their needs ... to be successful we must ensure that our organisational culture and working environment values everyone ... our workforce must reflect the area that we police and be equipped with the necessary skills, knowledge and attributes to deliver a professional service. In doing so we will be better able to meet the needs and expectations of everyone within the communities we serve'.

Prioritisation and "mainstreaming" – the Equality and Diversity Strategy 2008–2011 of the LSS states that the 'Society is committed to "mainstreaming" equality [in order] to promote diversity ... [placing] Equality and Diversity at the heart of carrying out its regulatory functions effectively and fairly'. To the LSS, the concept of mainstreaming 'means ensuring that:

- All staff take responsibility for Equality and Diversity issues.

- All managers know and meet their responsibilities to members of their team.

- All managers know and meet their responsibilities in relation to the provision of services.

- Council and Committee members are aware of Equality and Diversity and its implications (in terms of governance) for the decisions they make.

- Equality and Diversity are taken into account at the start of every new project.

- Equality and Diversity become a standard element of the criteria by which project and personal success are measured within the organisation.

- Equality and Diversity is simplified so that all staff can understand key implications and issues, and where necessary, identify where they need to ask for more technical assistance.

- We talk up diversity, emphasising its importance and benefits to the Society and profession, specific projects, and our general operations.

- Equality and Diversity is never viewed as solely the domain of Human Resources or a Diversity Officer.

"Mainstreaming" is the only way to ensure that diversity becomes a part of the way the Society functions rather than [as] an "initiative" or "project" which sits alongside existing Society work. This approach can mean progress is slower than it would otherwise be; with managers taking time to learn the necessary knowledge and skill and experiment putting them into practice, whereas a dedicated Diversity Officer could perhaps arrive at solutions or provide guidance immediately. Nevertheless, it is the only approach which creates the sustainability and accountability which is essential if diversity is to be meaningful within an organisation'.

The LSS goes on to state that 'if the goal of mainstreaming is to be achieved then it is essential that there is an overt link between Equality and Diversity and the strategic plan of the organisation. This link must be bi-directional. Equality and Diversity must always be taken account of in moves to achieve each of the organisation's overall strategic objectives, and key issues identified through Equality and Diversity must feed into the organisation's overall plan' and where necessary influence the direction and content of that plan.

The LSS also states that it believes in speaking openly and publicly about its equality work, sharing with others its experiences of implementation, successes and continuing challenges. The LSS states that it believes 'that open debate, a willingness to learn from others, and transparency about strengths and issues will progress the equality agenda further for all organisations'.

ATTITUDES AND VALUES

The implementation and performance management of the EDD Agenda, and the level of risk associated with it, will in part be a function of the attitudes and value sets of:

- the staff who are responsible for leadership, governance and championing, whether as principals, executives or team leaders, etc.;

- employees, agents, sub-contractors and suppliers (and especially those in customer or client service roles);

- clients, customers and those at whom service provision is targeted.

Critical value sets, such as those associated with the processes of prioritisation and mainstreaming, service provision, staff selection and management, ensuring compliance, risk assessment and resource allocation may be a function of:

- the processes of recruitment, training, socialisation and conditioning in the organisation;

- the relative effectiveness of processes of motivation, reward, sanction and punishment;

- the degree of congruence (or otherwise) between the beliefs of individuals, groups or teams, communities, managers and corporate staff;

- the relative strength of objective professional values as compared with personal or conventional attitudes and opinions.

Value sets and ingrained attitudes may be of particular significance in at least two sets of circumstances. In the first example, Deal and Kennedy describe high-risk activity types, such as those carried out by the uniformed, healthcare and social services, or high value client services, which are likely to be characterised by a rapid and significant level of feedback. Incidences of discrimination or of failures of compliance will, for example, be rapidly reported. There is then a potential for such events to assume crisis proportions, putting the organisation at an unpredictable and possibly uncontrollable level of negative comment, risk of loss of reputation, and damage.

In the second example, task-orientated activities, such as the provision of housing and welfare services to locally unpopular refugee or immigrant groups, which involve a wide variety of stakeholders and a critical degree of cross-functional sensitivity, may require a high level of collective or communal objectivity and professionalism on the part of the leaders and staff involved. It may be difficult for traditional mechanistic role cultures to achieve such a degree of professionalism and objectivity if they are characterised by entrenched patterns of conventional and ill co-ordinated behaviour, a strong degree of opinionation and an inability or unwillingness to change. Such task-oriented activities may also provide high power distance cultures with a dilemma. The necessary compliance with the Equality, Diversity and Discrimination Agenda may only be achieved in such types of organisation by direct enforcement (usually as a result of external legal intervention) and by the subsequent "punishment" of those staff or agents who are deemed to have "failed" in their duty. This may result in the accumulation in the organisation of resentment and hostility towards the statutory agenda for equality and discrimination, thereby creating counterproductive, countervailing and high risk forces that may resist necessary future processes of change.

EMOTIONAL INTELLIGENCE AND PROFESSIONAL COMPETENCE

The performance management of the EDD Agenda, and its associated risk, will also be a function of the *degree of objectivity,* the *freedom from opinionation,* the *emotional intelligence* and the *professional competence* that characterise the people and the organisation involved in the implementation of that agenda.

George and Goleman describe a variety of features of emotional intelligence. These include: (i) the need to develop awareness, understanding and empathy with moods and emotions in self and in others; and (ii) the need for sensitivity to employees and to clients, communities or customers in the external service or stakeholder environment. This emotional intelligence should underpin cognitive processes, create objectivity in decision-making, and thereby underpin the level of professional competence needed to deal with the potentially sensitive and sometimes controversial nature of the Equality, Diversity, Opportunity and Discrimination Agenda.

Morden suggests that such levels of professional competence are requisite to the application of the emotional intelligence concept in:

- Understanding non-routine, non-conventional, controversial, unexpected or unwanted situations to which the Equality and Discrimination Agenda may give rise.

- Decision-making about task or relationship-orientated behaviours appropriate to sensitive or emotionally complex situations associated with perceptions of unfair treatment or resource allocation, discrimination or harassment.

The achievement of a consistent performance management of the Equality, Diversity, Opportunity and Discrimination Agenda in the organisation may, however, be made unpredictable by the presence as managers, employees or agents, of principals or people characterised by any or all of:

- High power distance associated with strongly and entrenched conventional attitudes, in whom, in the case of men, there may for example still be a traditional resistance to developing or promoting women in the workplace or to employing gay men.

- Person-based or "Dionysian" cultures in which the organisation, its values and its service remit are perceived as the possession or preserve of powerful individuals who, by definition, operate and control according to their own opinions, attitudes and ambitions; and to whom the Equality and Opportunity Agenda may even pose a threat.

This in turn may be related to:

- Aggressive and strongly self-orientated Type "A" personalities, to whom, for instance, women, the disabled, people with mental health problems or the middle-aged may be perceived as weak or inadequate.

MANAGING PERFORMANCE AND ACHIEVING RESULTS

Performance management issues and the achievement of results are analysed in this section of Chapter 6. This part of the chapter looks at the processes of achieving compliance. It analyses EDD performance benchmarks and it deals with a variety of matters for management judgement.

Achieving compliance – compliance with the requisite EDD Agenda may take any one of at least three forms, as follow.

1. Internal enforcement traditionally based on reactive processes of:

    - The definition of the nature and scope of the principal, personal, vicarious or agency accountability required to comply with legislation or statutory regulation associated with the Equality, Diversity, Opportunity and Anti-Discrimination Agenda.

- Specific and prescriptive communication and training in what behaviour is required at the level of employer, employee, agent or service provider, etc.
- Enforcement by the application of rules, regulations, monitoring, audit and scrutiny, with onward reference to employee relations or disciplinary procedures and ultimately to threat of sanction, legal action or dismissal.

Such an approach to achieving compliance may be categorised as containing elements of Theory X, low trust, or immaturity approaches to management style (that is, see Morden, 2004, Chapters 3 and 12). This approach is likely to be characterised by inherent EDD Risk.

2. *Internal enforcement* based on *proactive processes* of the realignment of attitudes and values associated with the prioritisation and mainstreaming of the EDD Agenda. Such an approach might be categorised as containing elements of Theory Y or Theory Z, maturity, high trust and professionalised approaches to management style. The relevance to this approach of attitudes, values and emotional intelligence were described in earlier sections of this chapter. Issues of attitudinal and cultural change are dealt with in Chapter 7.

3. *External enforcement* where there are no effective internal mechanisms of achieving compliance. In such a case, a victim of discrimination or harassment may, for example, have little alternative in the UK to seeking the advice and assistance of employment lawyers. However, such advice

(and the actions that may follow from it) may then be subject to unpredictable contingent variables associated with any or all of:

- the personal wealth, status, opportunity and bargaining power of the individual concerned, relative to the employer;
- trade union bargaining power;
- the behaviour and dynamics of Employment Tribunals;
- the values and culture of the legal profession.

Performance benchmarks – where there is legislative, external, stakeholder or internal pressure on the organisation to demonstrate excellence or best practice in its performance management of the Equality, Diversity, Opportunity and Anti-Discrimination Agenda, there is likely to be a need to access and to make use of appropriate *performance benchmarks*.

These may be categorised as: (i) specific benchmarks of compliance; or (ii) generically applicable benchmarks relevant to the implementation of the EDD Agenda. Each is described below.

(i) *Specific UK benchmarks of compliance* – include:

- public sector Best Value Performance Indicators (BVPIs);

- the Equality Standard for Local Government (ESLG), described below;

- the findings of participant consultation and involvement processes to which reference has already been made above and which are required by the relevant Codes of Practice;

- the implications of the applicable case law.

The Equality Standard for Local Government (ESLG) – is, for example, applied by the ECFRS who note that the ESLG is 'a performance framework tool for continuous improvement [in] local authorities ... [and] to evidence how they provide a fair and equal service to all their customers'.

The ESLG describes itself as 'a tool to combat the institutional processes that lead to discrimination as part of the culture, administration and governance that can be found in many public organisations. Prevailing assumptions and practices can set up barriers that prevent fair access to services and equal employment opportunities, which in turn can discriminate against people ... Working with the Equality Standard will enable local authorities to mainstream equality, thereby ensuring that discriminatory barriers are identified and removed ... The Equality Standard provides a way of working within local authorities that makes the mainstreaming of equality into service delivery and employment an issue for all aspects of a local authority's work'.

The ESLG comments that the need for a proactive and systemic approach towards dealing with discrimination was underlined in the UK by the findings of the Stephen Lawrence Inquiry, published as The MacPherson Report in 1999, which highlighted the way in which institutional discrimination can influence how organisations operate and the manner in which services are provided by them.

The MacPherson Report defined institutional racism as a 'collective failure of an organisation to provide an appropriate and professional service to people because of their colour, culture, and ethnic origin. It can be detected in processes, attitudes and behaviour which amount to discrimination through ... prejudice, ignorance, thoughtlessness and racist stereotyping which disadvantage' ethnic groups or minorities.

The ESLG requires that systems and processes put in place to implement local government equality management should, *inter alia*, be:

- Committed to at a governance or corporate level, for example, using a personally accountable champion or equality steering group.

- Effectively led.

- Adapted to work within quality management systems.

- Inclusive of stakeholders and community, using a participative rather than a consultative strategy.

- Context-specific.

- Based on a co-ordinated, cross-functional and "whole authority" approach to service provision and employment.

- Be managed on a measurable outcome or result basis.

- Prepared to challenge existing arrangements, cultures and traditions. The ESLG notes that 'the aim of the Standard is to create a culture in which managers and staff will question and challenge assumptions about their services and re-assess them on the basis of equality and need'.

- Based on a continuous cycle of learning and improvement, for instance, using the process of impact assessment described in Chapter 8.

- Properly resourced. The ESLG states that it is necessary 'to consider resource levels as a part of the equality planning process'. The issue of resourcing and what is defined as "reasonable" have been analysed in previous chapters of this Short Guide.

- Scrutinised and validated on both an internal and an external basis, and be appropriate as a performance management system to the requirements of the national Comprehensive Performance Assessment (CPA) for local government authorities in the UK.

(ii) *Generically applicable benchmarks* relevant to the UK implementation of the EDD Agenda include:

- Public sector Best Value Performance Indicators (BVPIs).

- The UK Professional Associations Research Network (PARN) who, for instance, have selected the work of the Law Society of Scotland 'as an example of best practice for how a professional body can tackle' equality issues.

- The findings of the equality impact assessments described in Chapter 8.

- The European Foundation for Quality Management (EFQM) "Excellence Model".

- Six Sigma, described below.

Six Sigma – in which:

- generically specified variations from the norm;

- customer or client service satisfaction ratings;

- the degree of access to service providers, for instance, at the edge of service provision to what the ECFRS and the LSS describe as "hard to reach" or marginalised groups;

- opportunity ratings, whether employment or service-oriented; and

- the actual incidence of discrimination

may be driven by the performance management process from, say, 2σ (68.26 per cent) acceptable towards an ultimate goal of 6σ (99.73 per cent), at which point virtually all unacceptable types of performance variations (including costs of poor quality) will have been "squeezed out" of the organisation's employment record and its service provision.

Some issues for judgement – performance management is then likely to require the training or conditioning of managers, employees, agents and service providers in the consistent, formalised, standardised, emotionally intelligent and professionalised behaviour patterns to which reference has already been made in this chapter. Judgements will have to be made as to the appropriateness of behaviour patterns to context and circumstances. These might include situations where there is a predictably high potential risk of perceptions of discrimination or harassment, such as in the policing of or service provision to, or social care of "difficult", drug-addicted or hostile groups; the appointment of women to management posts; or the interaction with strongly traditional religious groups in which, for example, women or widows are habitually perceived as having second-class status or whose daughters are at risk of forced marriage. Other issues for judgement may include the following:

- The degree to which judgements about issues of compliance and performance management can be made in *absolute or relative terms* (or both). For instance, can interpersonal dynamics be standardised to a point where behaviours become consistently predictable, for instance, in the elimination of unwanted personal opinion or in the elimination of "incorrect" or "inappropriate'" language when dealing with specified or sensitive groups? This is a universalistic or a "one size fits all argument" widely applied to the uniformed services, educational, health or social care provision, and retail and customer services in the UK.

- The extent to which *varying degrees of compliance* can be permitted. One example might be the degree to which the expensive refurbishment of public or educational buildings and facilities is undertaken in order to meet the potential needs of the disabled (who may or may not then use them), thereby incurring substantial resource cost. Another example is the degree of tolerance of staff or agents who, however competent and valuable, are (as a matter of social conditioning, culture or personal opinion) irreversibly "programmed" to demonstrate discriminatory behaviour, for instance, towards women, certain ethnic minorities or castes, other faiths, the disabled, or homosexuals when unexpectedly confronted with non-routine or unpredictable situations outside of their normal job remit that are characterised by a high potential risk of discrimination or harassment.

POSTSCRIPT

This chapter has looked at the leadership and performance management of the EDD Agenda and of the EDD Risk associated with the implementation of that Agenda. The chapter was based on the analysis and inter-relationship of a series of key variables derived from a transactional and process-oriented approach to the analysis of leadership and management issues.

The Short Guide now moves on to describe the management of change in the application of the EDD Agenda. The purpose of seeking such change is two-fold. The first purpose is to reduce EDD Risk. The second purpose is to achieve significant and sustained enhancements in EDD performance, thereby, for instance, reducing costs of poor EDD quality.

(7) EDD Risk and Change Management

This chapter looks at issues of Equality, Diversity and Discrimination Risk from the viewpoint of the change management process. The chapter uses Lewin's force field analysis to explain the process of implementing change associated with the agenda for Equality, Diversity, Opportunity and Discrimination. It analyses issues of the perception, definition and understanding of change associated with the EDD Agenda. It looks at processes and forces that may resist change and lock, or freeze, the organisation into a risk-laden form. It then describes processes and forces that can be used to drive change, unlocking and moving the status quo towards a new or more acceptable specification, thereby reducing EDD Risk. The chapter concludes by making reference to professionalisation and to the concept of the "high trust" workplace as keys to the achievement of high levels of performance in organisations now more effectively aligned by the change management process with the values associated with the equality and diversity agenda.

The structure of this chapter is summarised in Figure 7.1.

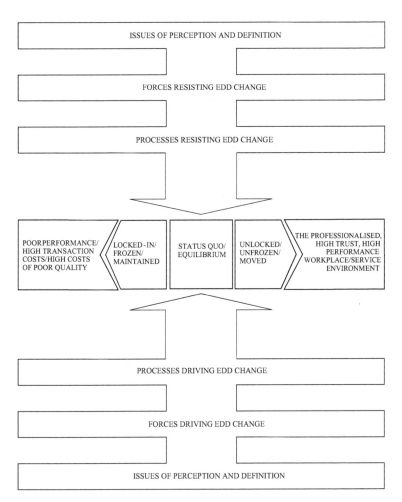

Figure 7.1   A change management process

ISSUES OF PERCEPTION AND DEFINITION

The need for change processes associated with the Equality, Opportunity, Diversity and Discrimination Agenda, and the risk associated with such change may be subject to varying individual, communal and organisational perceptions. One person's positive discrimination may be perceived by another to be negative or reverse. The experience of disability for one person may be seen as a source of expense to another, and so on.

Perception and definition comprise at least four inter-related *cognitive processes*. These are listed below.

Perception – in which a person becomes aware of, observes, or visualises an entity (or its attributes) using the mind or the senses, such that accumulated knowledge about this entity may then be subjected to the process of conceptualisation. For example, the particular work behaviour of employees suffering from severe stress or mental health disorders.

Conceptualisation – which involves the use of intellect, mental constructs, or the imagination in order to categorise and to fit perceptions and knowledge into a pattern, a classification or a scheme of things so that as a concept it may be subjected to interpretation. For example, the category of mental health disability in the workplace as a construct separate from physical disability.

Interpretation – which involves submitting perceptions and concepts to the process of explanation, comment, opinion, inference or judgement, for instance by making use of preconditioned or learned values, attitudes or cultures in order to create meaning. For example, how mental health disability can be related to the demands of the work environment within the context of disability legislation.

The derivation or establishment of meaning – by which interpretation and understanding take a particular form, significance, direction or intention. For example, how to prepare policies for, or to manage, people with mental health disabilities in the work environment.

Morden (2004) suggests that uncertainties associated with this cognitive process and the establishment of the values, thoughts and language which result from it could have at least four risk consequences for any change management process. These are:

Misunderstanding – where people involved simply do not understand what the change or its outcome are likely to mean, particularly if there has been ineffective communication between the proposer of the change and those who will be directly affected by it.

An installed base of thinking – described by Hamel and Prahalad as the maintenance of 'unquestioned conventions, a myopic view of opportunities and threats, and ... unchallenged precedents' that may make up an outmoded frame of reference.

Conflicting perceptions – in which different people assess and communicate the implications, equity, costs and benefits of change in different and potentially conflicting ways. Change may be resisted where people cannot agree on a definition of its character or its possible consequences for them. For example, an earlier chapter analysed some resource implications of the Equality, Diversity and Discrimination Agenda. It examined the concept of what was likely to be deemed "fair" or "reasonable" in that context. The chapter noted that perceptions of what was fair or reasonable might depend on the size or wealth of the organisation under consideration; or it might instead depend on how well informed people are about their rights and entitlements under the law and how able they are to fight for and to secure these rights. The problem of conflicting perceptions of what constitutes "fair shares for all" may, for example, find a particularly difficult manifestation in the three following issues. The first is the justification of differential pay rates, such as those made to women in the UK, for equal work. The second is the relevance of spent conviction to the recruitment and employment of former prisoners. The third is the process of ensuring the proper provision of public, educational, welfare or policing services to women and children from ethnic communities, described in earlier chapters, that are characterised by high levels of traditionally male-dominated or historically orthodox culture and behaviour in which there is extremely low trust or tolerance of "outsiders", or the state.

A lack of trust in the proponents of the change – such that planned programmes of change are rejected by those likely to be affected.

RIGHTS, ENTITLEMENTS AND RESPONSIBILITIES

Organisations, principals, employees, agents, service providers, clients and customers all have rights, entitlements, and responsibilities in respect of the Equality, Diversity and Discrimination Agenda. An issue under this heading is: (i) the extent to which these rights, entitlements, and responsibilities are clearly defined and understood; or instead (ii) the degree to which there is room for variation and interpretation under different contexts. The matter may become complicated where it is likely that the final arbiter in any particular case will be a legal one. Earlier chapters noted that in such circumstances the nature of the outcome may be subject to the contingencies of the values of legal specialists, and the perceptions and behaviour of Employment Tribunals or the courts.

PERCEPTIONS OF REQUISITE COMPLIANCE AND PERFORMANCE

Chapter 6 noted that issues for judgement in respect of the risks associated with Equality, Diversity and Discrimination Agenda included:

- The degree to which issues of required compliance or performance may be conceptualised in *absolute* or *relative terms* (or both). It gave the example of the standardisation of interpersonal behaviour, for instance, in the context of employment or service architectures.

- The degree to which *varying degrees of compliance or performance* may be permissible. It gave the example of the reaction of staff potentially likely to demonstrate discriminatory behaviour, such as that frequently directed to the physically or mentally disabled, in unexpected, non-routine, high-pressure or unpredictable situations outside of their job remit that contain a high risk of discrimination, harassment or legal sanction. Another example might be the behaviour of new immigrants who are as yet unaware of UK expectations in the matter, such as in the reaction of males to female customer service representatives or members of the uniformed services who are in the process of carrying out their legitimate duties, providing assistance or enforcing the law.

ACCOMMODATION OR COMPROMISE

The issue of unpredictable or varying perceptions may ultimately result in uncertainties about the meaning of, or potential for any, or all of the following:

- The *accommodation* of, or coming to terms with different viewpoints or interpretations of statutory duty, codes of practice or expected behaviours.

- The degree of acceptable *variation*, such as: (i) in the stated capability (such as language) required to carry out a particular activity; (ii) in the objective standard of achievement of any given outcome; or (iii) in the tolerance of covert discriminatory behaviour, for instance, towards married female employees with children or those with alternative sexual orientation.

- The establishment of mutually acceptable, "reasonable" or legally justifiable *compromise*, for instance, in the employment of the disabled (who may not be able to fulfil all of the requirements of a role description that has been job evaluated at a particular point on a salary scale) or in the use of differential pay systems in which the principle of equal pay for equal work is for whatever reason not applied.

FORCES RESISTING EDD CHANGE

There are a variety of *forces* that may have the potential to restrain or to resist the implementation of EDD change. Such forces may maintain, lock-in or "freeze" the existing status quo, thereby giving rise to EDD Risk. Some of these forces are summarised below.

Apathy – in which people in work or service environments: (i) neither understand nor want to understand the relevance or priority to them and to the organisation of the Equality, Diversity, Opportunity and Discrimination Agenda; nor; (ii) for instance, for reasons of the strong Anglo-Saxon characteristics of individualism, self-opinionation, self-reference or personal self-absorption, described in an earlier chapter, care in any way about such "inconvenient" matters.

Inertia – for instance, caused by a long time period during which the organisation and its staff have not been affected by the need for significant change. A long-established workforce may be strongly antipathetic to such a need for change. Resistance to change may be strengthened where there are older managers and staff who have only a few years to go before retirement. Similarly, strongly collectivised and cohesive groups of staff, such as members of fire and rescue service watches or military staff held together by the strong bonds generated by battlefield conditions, could potentially be in a position to thwart those parts of the Equality, Diversity and Discrimination Agenda to which they take exception. The training and deployment by US armed forces of black recruits into flying duties (particularly as fighter pilots) was only achieved during the Second World War after direct government intervention and insistence.

Inertia is related to *a preference for stability and a low tolerance of change* – which is a natural human reaction. The prospect of change and disruption to well-established ways of operating may, at the very least, be inconvenient to all concerned. At worst, as in the case of some hasty 1980s and 1990s exercises in positive discrimination in respect of the promotion of women to managerial posts in long-established manufacturing companies in the UK, conditions of change may become associated with a high degree of disruption to working patterns and resultant occupational stress to all concerned. Matters under this heading may be exacerbated where there are any or all of the following.

Entrenched attitudes, custom and practice, habit and conformity – in which people have (perhaps because of an installed base of thinking already described above) become habituated to doing things in certain ways, irrespective of their appropriateness to the Equality, Diversity and Discrimination Agenda. Custom and practice become easy and convenient to those who are familiar with it. Long-established habits may then be hard to break, as in the case of the limiting of management or professional recruitment to ethnic or social elites (such as the Spanish or the Portuguese in Central and South America), or to "Ivy League"-type universities, or to unreformed and restrictive professional bodies, thereby reducing opportunity.

Personal and collective opinion – in which there is the introduction of strong self or collective opinionation, particularly at the level of governance and senior or line management that is incongruent with, or actively hostile to the values and attitudes associated with the Equality, Diversity, Opportunity and Discrimination Agenda. The dissemination of such opinion may in value judgement terms be categorised as cynical and unprofessional as well as subjective within the context of the workplace or the service environment, aimed as it is at undermining or sabotaging the fulfilment of the statutory, ethical or social responsibilities of the organisation.

Fear of conflict – in which, for instance, those people charged with leading the change agenda are, for whatever reason (whether personal, cultural, positional, political or otherwise), unable or unwilling to make, to implement or to enforce decisions that will bring them into direct conflict with others.

Stigma – as a result of which, for instance, the disabled or those with alternative sexual orientations suffer personal, social or organisational discrimination. In its UK campaign to fight the widespread discrimination faced by people with mental health problems, "Time to Change" describes mental health issues:

- As still being 'surrounded by ignorance, fear, and prejudice, despite the fact that around one in four adults will experience them at some point in their lives'.

- As remaining 'a lingering taboo' in which 'people affected by mental health problems experience stigma and discrimination. Shame and stigma wreck lives'.

- As giving rise to an experience in which 'the impact of prejudice, ignorance and fear ... can be devastating for people, families, communities and society. Stigma may prevent people seeking help when they need it (and) it stops people with ability getting the jobs they are qualified to do'.

Such stigma may drive the deep-seated resentment of, or open hostility, towards people at whom the Equality, Diversity and Discrimination Agenda is directed. At worst, it may lead to the kind of disability hate crime described in Chapter 1.

Inappropriate values and culture – in which the wider personal and organisational values and priorities of decision-makers may be incongruent with the needs of change. Strongly entrenched, self-absorbed, inward-looking or "group think"-type cultures, for instance, may simply not accept the value or priority of an agenda, such as that of equality and opportunity, as being in any way relevant to the strategy and operations of the enterprise. Much debate has, for example, centred on the apparently "macho", aggressive and bonus-driven culture of male staff in the UK and US financial services sectors and the relationship of that culture to the recent failures in those sectors. Opponents of the male-dominated behaviour that is purported to characterise the financial services sector argue that the presence of more women in senior management positions might have calmed the febrile atmosphere being generated, and mitigated some of the worst consequences of that behaviour. Masculine cultures were described in Chapter 4.

Ineffective styles of leadership or management – failures or weakness of leadership or governance, a lack of the necessary commitment, an inability or unwillingness to champion and to bring about change, or an ineffective style of management may all contribute to the failure of implementation of an Equality, Diversity, Opportunity or Anti-Discrimination Agenda and give rise to EDD Risk.

So, for instance, the authors of the Bain Review stated that, at the time of the report's publication in 2002, the UK Fire and Rescue Service (FRS) had been characterised by a poor record of staff management. It commented that policy, procedures and practice in the Fire and Rescue Service gave cause for concern and that 'despite clear policies from management and the Fire Brigades' Union in favour of diversity, only lip-service was in practice paid at the time to the equality agenda. Harassment and bullying in the service were then described as being 'too prevalent'. The Bain Review concluded that 'leadership must recognise that urgent action' was required to deal with the situation as the report's authors perceived it.

A subsequent Audit Commission report identified management issues as a key theme for modernisation in the Fire and Rescue Service, and concluded that in order to make progress on diversity issues a change in culture, attitude and behaviour was required. This change was seen to be most necessary at the senior management level and was later identified by the UK government's Office of the Deputy Prime Minister (ODPM) as a key issue for staff development in the FRS.

Perceptions of negative or reverse discrimination – Morden notes that 'the use of programmes or policies of positive discrimination or affirmative action' (such as those described in Chapter 5 of this Short Guide) 'may result in perceptions on the part of majority employee groups of negative or reverse discrimination on the part of their employer. These perceptions may result from the collective emergence of a view that the proactive favouring of one group is taking place at the expense of another group. Or, instead, there may be a belief that one group is being favoured at everyone's expense and that enterprise performance is being sub-optimised as a result.

Charges of negative discrimination may carry most weight where it has become obvious to all that the operational performance of the favoured individual or group is clearly less effective (despite training, etc.) than what would have been expected from the group that now claims to be being discriminated against by the programme of affirmative action. Similarly, charges of negative discrimination are likely to arise when an employer hires or promotes a member of a favoured group over an equally (or better) qualified candidate who is not a member of that favoured group.

The need to respond to charges of negative discrimination may place management in a difficult position, particularly if the enterprise is fully committed to a programme of affirmative action. One strategy will be to ensure that those individuals who are being positively favoured are: (i) absolutely clear about the performance levels expected of them (and properly equipped to achieve them); and (ii) clearly understand that their performance will be evaluated, rewarded or criticized in exactly the same way as everybody else in that occupational category.

Visible positive results (preferably showing up in the "bottom line") are the best way of overcoming the potential reaction to perceptions of negative discrimination on the part of key majority groups'.

PROCESSES RESISTING EDD CHANGE

The *process* of resisting the implementation of the Equality, Diversity, Opportunity and Discrimination Agenda, and the risk to which this resistance gives rise, may be based on any or all of the generic forms described below.

A refusal to contemplate new experiences and new ways of working, or a fear of the unknown – in which change is perceived "as an unknown quantity" and as such must be rejected or resisted, whatever this implies for EDD Risk.

Denial – in which there is a refusal to admit to any particular need for change or a refusal to accept the nature of the agenda under consideration, or a refusal to accept any appropriate definition such that it is impossible to agree the nature of any solution. Such denial may, for example, characterise organisations that have failed to plan ahead and to make proper long-term budgetary provision for the implementation of the EDD Agenda and then claim that they are not in a position to meet their immediate statutory responsibilities because they have no funds available for the purpose.

The protection of self-interest – in which, for instance, powerful or majority groups resist change agendas that threaten their self-interest, status, prestige or job security. The entrenched habit of recruiting graduates from élite universities, such as the Grandes Ecoles, means that employment opportunities in management have very much been maintained in favour of the white middle classes in France and effectively denied to other groups.

Aggressive behaviour – in which individuals or groups direct aggressive, hostile or Type "A" behaviour towards those people who, despite being charged with implementing a change agenda, are: (i) characterised by the fear of interpersonal conflict described in an earlier section, above; or (ii) find themselves in a weak bargaining position.

Ritualised behaviour – in which, for example: (i) use is made of formal rules, procedures and committee structures to block or dissipate the momentum for change; (ii) repeated use is made of bureaucratic or upward hierarchical referral to slow or to water down change processes; or (iii) change issues are referred to possibly lengthy or complex negotiating procedures in which management representatives, trade unions, staff associations or mediators become involved in a process whose outcome is likely to be long-drawn-out, uncertain and unpredictable.

Direct opposition, whether overt or covert – by which the momentum for change is directly challenged by the use of countervailing power, for instance, based upon ownership, status, access to political decision-makers, group solidarity, culture, history and tradition, or prestige. Reference to such countervailing power was made in Chapters 5 and 6.

FORCES DRIVING EDD CHANGE

EDD change may be *driven* or caused by a variety of influences, which may have the effect of unlocking, unfreezing or moving the existing status quo. These forces may be external or internal. Each is analysed below.

EXTERNAL DRIVERS OF EDD CHANGE

External drivers of change in the EDD Agenda include any or all of the following:

- changing government policy, legislation and regulation;

- changing social attitudes towards what is perceived as fair, required, reasonable or acceptable public behaviour in matters of equality, opportunity or disability;

- the need to manage in a legally, ethically and socially responsible manner;

- the need to manage diversity and opportunity in a multicultural or polyglot society in which any form of discrimination is seen as undesirable and unacceptable.

EXTERNAL REFERENCE

The process of change associated with the Equality, Diversity, Opportunity and Discrimination Agenda may instead be informed or shaped by such forms of external reference as:

- Influential public reports, such as the UK's MacPherson (1999) or the Bain (2002).

- External benchmarks, such as the UK Best Value Performance Indicators (BVPI), Comprehensive Performance Assessment (CPA), Risk Management Plans, Equality Standards for Local Government (ESLG); Six Sigma; or those benchmarks associated with the European Foundation for Quality Management (EFQM) "Excellence Model", to which reference was made in Chapter 6.

- Ongoing public initiatives, such as the UK "Time To Change" campaign against mental health discrimination or the implementation of "zero-tolerance" policies towards racism, disability hate crime, forced marriage, etc.

INTERNAL DRIVERS OF EDD CHANGE

Internal drivers of change may derive from the external pressures described above. Those pressures are then likely to be focused on internal issues of performance management described in earlier chapters associated with:

- leadership and governance;

- changing internal attitudes, values and culture;

- the nature of what are deemed to be appropriate behaviours and appropriate levels of achievement;

- the perception that the costs, or costs of poor quality, associated with EDD infringement are no longer acceptable;

- the pursuit of levels of EDD performance that may objectively be deemed to be "excellent" when compared with external benchmarks. Such levels of achievement are increasingly required of public sector organisations and large private sector companies in the UK.

PROCESSES DRIVING EDD CHANGE

A variety of internal EDD change processes may be identified. The application of these processes may have the effect of moving the status quo or establishing it in a new or modified form. They are summarised as follows.

THE APPLICATION OF CAPABILITY AND COMPETENCE-BASED METHODOLOGIES

It may be the case that the greater is the reliance placed by the organisation on capability and competence-based performance management, the less likely it will be that problems of Equality, Diversity, Opportunity or Discrimination will occur. Staff are selected, trained, managed and assessed on the basis of objective performance behaviours and outcomes. They are then paid to achieve outcomes that can only be delivered by the exercise of these behaviours and capabilities. Either they are competent or they are not. Those that cannot reach the required performance levels are assisted through further training and development or their employment is terminated. In this respect they enjoy the same rights as everyone else and they must demonstrate the same responsibilities to their employer and to their customers or clients in the service environment.

The Law Society of Scotland (LSS), for instance, comments that 'our exploration of faiths has led us to consider the attributes [that] lawyers bring to their work above and beyond what is provided by formal education and training'. These attributes might include openness to new or different ideas, attitudes to the "conventional wisdoms" described in an earlier section, and the nature of interpersonal skills. The LSS has proposed competency-based performance management and appraisal, linked to formal schemes of job analysis, job evaluation and equal pay structures. It has also proposed to add competency-based training relating to issues of equality and diversity to client core programmes in solicitors' offices in Scotland.

THE RECRUITMENT PROCESS

Employment policies and practices in the organisation will need to be seen to deliver equality and opportunity in a demonstrably fair manner. The LSS categorises such an approach to recruitment and selection as being "merit-based".

Such merit-based recruitment policies might call for the use of anonymous objective and competency-based testing of candidates, perhaps carried out at arm's length. "Neutral" recruitment and selection processes might also be used. The LSS has suggested a neutral policy that meets equality and opportunity requirements. All "identifying" data is removed from candidate applications or work portfolios used in short-listing. Such a process also removes data: (i) on institutions at which qualifications were achieved; and (ii) on past employment record. The process instead requires "relevant" and provable data on the candidate's past work experience and his or her capability and competence. This might be based on work portfolios that have been objectively verified and officially validated by an outside agency, for instance, at the expense of the employer or the candidate, or both. This means that the process of short-listing applicants contains less emphasis on the background of candidates. It may mean that assumptions made on the basis: (i) of social class or background; (ii) of where applicants went to school or university; or (iii) easily identifiable maternity/disability-related gaps in employment history are less likely to influence the recruitment process.

Alternatively, the recruitment process might be based on assessment centre-based techniques of capability analysis, case study, examination, role-play, presentational process, etc., carried out at arm's length and reported against justifiable generic and professional outcomes (for example, professional, verbal and communication skills; speed and accuracy of work; ability to work under pressure; interpersonal skills; objectivity; analysis, etc.). This would have to be carried out by accredited sub-contractors, for instance, on behalf of a trade, profession or sector and on a collective basis. The process might be carried out at given "levels", for example, undergraduate, professional, supervisory, junior management, middle management, senior management, etc. Such a process would, however, raise the issue of cost. Who would bear the cost and would applicants be required to pay fees as in the case of the MBA GMAT, perhaps redeemable against subsequent salary or income tax?

Whatever the process used, the critical importance of the recruitment process to the Equality, Diversity, Opportunity and Discrimination Agenda means that it is likely to be subject to close scrutiny. The Essex County Fire and Rescue Service (ECFRS), for instance, notes that 'nationally, Fire and Rescue Services report on recruitment, retention, and progression of employees in relation to gender, ethnicity, and disability'.

EDD TRAINING PROCESS

There will be a need to provide employees and agents with appropriate knowledge, training, skills and motivation relevant to the implementation of the Equality and Diversity Agenda, and relevant to the avoidance of discrimination. The ECFRS, for example, 'recognises the importance of training staff in relation to our duties … and ensuring staff have the skills and understanding to challenge inappropriate behaviour and help to eliminate … unlawful discrimination'.

Training could include (in an *increasing order of complexity*) any or all of the following:

- equality, equal opportunity and diversity type training; or more specifically

- the role and relevance of the Equality, Diversity and Discrimination Agenda in the organisation; and

- understanding the necessities and benefits of equality and diversity (for example, in service provision); and

- awareness and understanding of the relevant legislation and its implications; to include

– analysis and understanding of the categories of equality, diversity and discrimination; and

– awareness and understanding of different types of discrimination and their costs and implications.

Then:

- definition and allocation of responsibilities and their operational or service implications;

- relevant communication training in respect of critical professional or high-value sales or customer service interactions which require a significant degree of language clarity and sophistication on the part of those involved in their delivery;

- training in cultural awareness and understanding, culture-specific issues;

- cross-cultural communication and inter-relationships;

- performance management implications;

- training in impact assessment and risk analysis;

- organisational values and culture awareness;

- understanding implications for processes of employee socialisation and conditioning;

- training for potential and actual promotees;

- concepts and implications of positive discrimination or affirmative action, and negative or reverse discrimination;

- awareness and understanding of critical professional and service impacts;

- strategic management and governance implications, for example, in terms of the Voice of the Customer, capability, value generation or value chain issues, internal and external architectures including agency relationships, external and political relationships, implications for personal and corporate reputation, etc.

Appropriate training for those principals, agents or stakeholders involved in the process of corporate governance is likely to be essential.

Decisions will have to be made as to whether such EDD training may be purchased from or delivered by external sources, or whether it should be custom-specified and produced in-house. Decisions will also have to be made as to whether such training is to be optional or is instead made mandatory and validated, especially where: (i) it relates to individual and organisational capability, and assessment; or (ii) has statutory implications.

PROCESSES OF SOCIALISATION AND CONDITIONING

The strength of positive communal and professional values associated with the Equality, Diversity, Opportunity and Discrimination Agenda may be a function of the degree to which such values have been embedded by processes of socialisation and conditioning in the organisation.

The objective of the use of these processes of socialisation and conditioning is so to establish and to reinforce desirable communal and professional values that, in performance management terms, there is: (i) the achievement of appropriate and positive changes in behaviour; (ii) the establishment of high levels of interpersonal and intra-organisational trust; and as a result (iii) high levels of performance, perhaps indicated by criteria of excellence where these are applicable.

Socialisation and conditioning may, over time, make use of any or all of the following processes, some of which have already been analysed in this or earlier chapters:

- leadership and championing;

- external reference and benchmarking;

- illustration and example;

- the use of knowledge management methodologies to convert relevant tacit knowledge and experience (such as in the application of emotional intelligence to cross-cultural interaction) into explicit and directly useable communal paradigms;

- training;

- implementation and repetition;

- review and reinforcement;

- reward for compliance;

- sanction for non-compliance;

- promotion and the careful prior preparation of promotion candidates;

- the termination of the employment or contracts of staff or agents who, after being given the appropriate opportunities to comply, remain unable or unwilling to conform to the required attitudes and behaviours that result from the change process.

The objective of such processes of socialisation and conditioning is to achieve a changed culture in which there is habitually predictable and positive governance and behaviour in respect of the Equality, Diversity, Opportunity and Discrimination Agenda, whether internally or in the service environment. This habitual and predictable positive behaviour may then in EDD performance management terms take the organisation to the status of "high trust" efficiency described by Fukuyama, in which the workplace can be organised 'on a more flexible and group-oriented basis, with more responsibility delegated to lower levels of the organisation'. Fukuyama suggests that the development of high efficiency, high trust workplaces 'requires habituation to the ... norms of community, and the acquisition of virtues like loyalty, honesty, integrity, and dependability. The group ... has to adopt [these] common norms of community as a whole before trust can become generalized among its members'.

PROFESSIONALISATION, PERFORMANCE AND THE HIGH TRUST WORKPLACE

The change process associated with the EDD Agenda may have as an ultimate objective the creation of a professionalised, high trust, quality-oriented and productive organisation. This is analysed overleaf.

PROFESSIONALISATION

The effective professionalisation of the processes of EDD leadership and management may lead to the embedding throughout the organisation, and at all levels, of behaviours that are any or all of:

- informed about the EDD Agenda;

- de-opinionated, objective and consistent;

- emotionally intelligent;

- impact and risk aware;

- task, relationship and outcome-orientated;

- service-oriented;

- properly delegated, monitored and controlled;

- consistent, predictable and reliable;

- cost, quality and value aware.

PERFORMANCE MANAGEMENT, EFFICIENCY AND EFFECTIVENESS

The change process associated with the EDD Agenda may in performance management terms have as an ultimate objective the creation of effectiveness and efficiency at all levels of the organisation and its relationship architecture, such that the internalisation of the agenda into mainstream values and process implies:

- the full exercise of rights, entitlements and responsibilities by all parties concerned;

- expectations of consistent and high levels of performance from all, relative to the remuneration and reward system being applied;

- the refusal to accept under-performance from any employee, any agent or any stakeholder, at whatever level;

- the refusal to accept behaviours in the work or service environment that are characterised by hostility to or non-compliance with the Equality, Diversity, Opportunity and Discrimination Agenda, whatever is the source or reason for this hostility or non-compliance;

- the refusal in the work or service environment to accept behaviours characterised by excessive individualism or unnecessary opinionation;

- the non-acceptance of unnecessary transaction costs or costs of poor service quality associated with failures of compliance with the agenda or with statutory duties associated therewith.

THE HIGH TRUST WORKPLACE

Fukuyama suggests that the most effective organisations are based on communities of shared values and attitudes. For example, the ECFRS states that, across all strands of equality, its aim is 'to work towards a values-based culture, in which dignity and respect for [others] is central to how we work, and [is] evident [from] our policies, actions and behaviour'.

Fukuyama comments that such communities do not require extensive contractual or legal regulation of their relationships and architectures because an established consensus gives members of the group a basis for mutual trust. Fukuyama states that 'if people who have to work together in an enterprise trust each other because they are all operating according to a common set of ethical norms, doing business costs less. Such a society will be better able to innovate organisationally, since the high degree of trust will permit a wide variety of social relationships to emerge ... by contrast, people who do not trust one another will end up co-operating only under a system of formal rules and regulations, which have to be negotiated, agreed to, litigated, and enforced [if necessary by coercive means]. This legal apparatus, serving as a substitute for trust, entails ... "transaction costs". Widespread distrust in a society, in other words, imposes a kind of tax on all forms of economic activity, a tax that high trust societies do not have to pay'. Within the context of the Equality and Diversity Agenda, such transaction costs have been described in this Short Guide to include any or all of the following:

- The costs of holding together organisations, agencies, architectures and value chains that are neither characterised by agreed values, trust or compliance. Such costs include mechanisms of governance, regulation and control within the management process and the specification of contractual agreements within the organisation.

- The costs of finding trustworthy employees, agents or suppliers.

- The costs of negotiating and enforcing contracts within external service or supply architectures.

- The costs of ensuring or enforcing compliance with statutory regulation.

- The costs of dealing with non-compliance, discrimination or malpractice.

- Other generic costs of poor quality.

POSTSCRIPT

This chapter has looked at ways in which the change management process may be used to lessen EDD Risk and to enhance organisational performance. Key outcomes of change in EDD management may then include greater professionalism, increased trust and reduced costs of poor quality.

The Short Guide now moves on to Chapter 8. That final chapter describes some practical strategies by which EDD Risk itself may be categorised and managed. The chapter then suggests what might happen in the event of an outright failure to deal with EDD Risk and concludes that, as a consequence, such risk needs to be properly understood and dealt with at a strategic level within the organisation.

(8) EDD Risk Management Strategies

This chapter describes a variety of practical strategies by which EDD Risk may be managed and reduced, and opportunity encouraged. The chapter then deals with the potential for EDD crisis and concludes by reiterating the need for a strategic view of the formulation and implementation of the EDD Agenda. The chapter builds on the analysis of types and sources of EDD Risk given in the preceding chapters of this Short Guide.

EDD RISK ANALYSIS

Some examples of the consequences of inequality and discrimination were given in Chapter 1 of this Short Guide. Some key types of EDD Risk were described in Chapter 2. A variety of sources of EDD Risk were identified and analysed in Chapters 3 to 5. The need for effective EDD Risk appraisal, performance and change management was described in Chapters 6 and 7.

CATEGORISING EDD RISK

EDD Risk may be categorised in a number of ways. Some examples are given below.

The degree of importance or seriousness – which might be described on a continuum ranging from: (i) minor infringement, easily dealt with by administrative procedures; through to (ii) serious problems of internal or service compliance which have the potential to lead to disciplinary action or dismissal; to (iii) critical or systemic failures likely to lead to legal action, loss of contracts, costs of compensation, threat to governance and organisational reputation, full-blown crisis or external intervention as may occur in the public sector.

The Voice of the Customer (VOC), *client approval or customer service ratings* – which ratings may range from the highly positive to the completely negative. For example, the provision and maintenance of public sector rented housing.

Underperformance – in which substandard operational performance by any individual employee or group, categorised in Chapter 2, presents an EDD Risk to the organisation in either or both of the employment or service arenas. The process of dealing with alleged underperformance may itself lead to charges of discrimination, even if roles, responsibilities and required capabilities have all been clearly formalised and communicated.

Timescale of EDD Risk – which is based on Elliot Jaques' *Time-Span of Discretion* methodology, in which risk and time span are related. The more serious the risk: (i) the longer will be the timescale of its impact; and (ii) the longer and the more expensive in resource and reputational terms will be its resolution. For example, the long-term impact on the UK Police and Fire and Rescue Services of the MacPherson and the Bain Reports described in Chapters 6 and 7.

IMPACT ASSESSMENT

Impact assessment is a formal process of ongoing monitoring and review by the organisation:

- To identify the impact, effect or risk associated with the implementation of the EDD Agenda within employment and service environments.

- To identify whether such impacts are positive, or instead adverse or negative. Adverse or negative impacts may result from the implementation of policies that contain differential and unjustifiable effects on the various equality groups to which they refer. For example, recruitment policies that have the effect of favouring some groups and disadvantaging others.

- To ensure that action is taken to eliminate or to reduce negative or adverse impacts on any particular group.

There are two types of impact assessment, as follow:

- *Retrospective assessments* – in which the consequences of past and present EDD policies are identified. The organisation would be expected to learn from its experience and to improve its future EDD performance.

- *Predictive assessments* – in which the potential future effects of EDD policies and plans are evaluated before they are implemented. For example, housing, welfare and healthcare provision in locations of rapid immigration or the build-up of populations of asylum seekers.

RISK MANAGEMENT STRATEGIES

This section describes a number of risk management strategies that may be applied to the Agenda for Equality, Diversity, Opportunity and Discrimination.

Risk reduction – Chapters 6 and 7 identified a variety of strategies by which the organisation might reduce its EDD Risk. For instance, reference was made to the careful selection and conditioning of governance, management, staff and agents to internalise and commit to the consistent and predictable delivery of professionalised behaviours appropriate to the implementation of the equality and opportunity agenda.

Identifying and communicating the cost of poor quality and the "hidden factory" – the risks of loss of value or reputation described in earlier chapters have, *inter alia*, been categorised in terms of EDD Risk as costs of poor quality (COPQ) under Six Sigma methodology. Such costs result from nonconformance with the standards or benchmarks associated with the performance or change management of the Equality, Diversity, Opportunity and Discrimination Agenda, described in Chapters 6 and 7. Costs relevant to the EDD Agenda have already been described to include:

- unnecessary costs of compliance and enforcement, whether internal or external;

- unnecessary costs of legal and remedial action, whether internal or external;

- the financial and resource opportunity cost represented by the organisation's "hidden factory" (or *secondary capability*) which is required to identify and to fix unwanted problems associated with failures of leadership, implementation and management process. The hidden factory as a source of unnecessary cost represents a net consumer or destroyer of value.

Co-operation, partnership and integration – reference has already been made in earlier chapters to circumstances in which organisations must of necessity work within agent or partnership-based relationship architectures. In such situations, the process of EDD management will seek to ensure a consistent level of compliance by all stakeholders with statute, case law and reasonable expectations.

Reference has also been made in previous chapters to public sector procurement being used as a form of leverage on private sector suppliers to raise the overall level of EDD compliance and performance management throughout the political economy.

Target hardening – by which there is a proactive reduction of the vulnerability of critical activities to risk. This might include quota-based recruitment that is proportionate to population characteristics, as sometimes practiced in Canada. It might instead mean the very careful screening, conditioning, motivation and supervision of staff involved in "front-line" tasks associated with service provision. The performance of such types of task will be restricted only to those people judged to be properly trained and suited to the demands of the work, whether it be in the uniformed services, in the provision of health or social services, in the determination of patterns of client service to sensitive groups (such as the elderly or children at risk) or in the provision of high-value customer services (such as those associated with finance or transportation).

Risk avoidance – by which the organisation proactively or deliberately identifies and avoids certain types of EDD Risk. This strategy could take such forms as:

- Separating out high-risk categories from the general service environment, for instance, by relocating families at risk of disability hate crime into safe and secure accommodation.

- Espousing aggressive zero tolerance policies against any form of discriminatory behaviour in the work or service environment. Employers and service providers will make it abundantly clear that all incidences of abuse will, without exception, be pursued or prosecuted.

- The seeking of locations characterised by a homogeneous rather than a polyglot or multicultural population. This strategy has been used by Far Eastern multinationals who may prefer to locate in conditions that mirror their experience at home. This issue was also dealt with in an earlier chapter.

Log keeping – by which detailed formal records and minutes are kept of all sensitive forms of interaction, whether internally (that is, in selection or promotion decisions, or in staff appraisal) or externally in respect of service provision. Such log keeping is now a standard feature of the UK public sector and an essential part of the human resource management process.

Media management – by which the enterprise maintains co-operative, proactive or transparent relationships with the media, assisting that media during times of internal difficulty rather than attempting to hide, evade or deny its responsibilities. This strategy is related to *crisis management*, below.

EDD CRISIS MANAGEMENT

External pressure groups or the media may identify failures of EDD implementation, or worse, discover actual failures of compliance by the organisation. Such pressure groups or media may then interpret these shortcomings in whatever way that suits their own interests or agendas. *So may an EDD crisis be created* (that is, see Morden, 2007, Chapter 10).

The EDD Agenda provides fertile ground from which to harvest such a crisis and from which to generate publicity, whether positive, negative or damaging. This is because:

- The EDD concept may easily be *simplified*, for instance, in the form of 'inequality bad; failures of compliance worse'.

- The EDD concept is at the same time *technically complex*, for instance, in legal, behavioural or medical terms. People may therefore look for simplified "explanations" or stereotypes in the absence of objective explanations. For example, 'it's all because men still hate promoting women to management positions'. Such a statement, while emotive, can neither be proven nor disproven. It all depends on your prejudice.

- The EDD concept is *data rich*. There is plenty of information available, so any number of interpretations or opinions are possible. For example, 'the evidence shows that most gays are subjected to harassment and discrimination at some point during their working lives'. Again, such a statement cannot easily be proven or disproved.

- There may be no *absolute answers* to EDD questions. It may all depend on the situation, particularly where a pragmatic and contingency-based view is taken towards the formulation of EDD statute and case law, as in the UK. For example, there can probably never be an absolute resolution to the opportunity and excellence dilemma described in Chapter 5. For instance, the Emperor Napoleon founded the first of the now famous Grandes Ecoles because the French universities of the time were not capable of delivering the vocational types and quality of military, engineering and administrative expertise he needed to expand and run his empire. The graduates (*les cadres*) of such "schools of excellence" have an undoubted and formidably successful performance record, particularly in rescuing the post-1945 French economy from its wartime devastation and placing it at the heart of the European Union.

- The EDD Agenda is prone to *sloganising*. The crisis may be encapsulated and communicated in a few choice and telling words, to which there may no qualification attached. For example, 'racist police behave like thugs in quelling immigrant riot'.

- The process of implementing and managing the EDD Agenda will always (as an unqualifiable generalisation) be subject to the workings of *Murphy's Law*. That is, if something can go wrong, it will go wrong; and the media or special interest groups involved will always find out when it does.

THE STRATEGIC MANAGEMENT OF EDD RISK

The implementation of the EDD Agenda and the performance management of EDD Risk is the subject of this Guide as a whole. This chapter has identified specific strategies by which to deal with that risk.

The processes of the identification and management of EDD Risk that are the subject of this Guide are *strategic*. It has been the contention of the author throughout that EDD Risk can only be dealt with if it is the subject of systematic strategic management, committed governance and leadership, prioritisation or mainstreaming, and effective management and motivation at the level of implementation. There is likely to be little or no alternative as social and political pressures for equality and opportunity strengthen, and the sanctions for non-compliance become more aggressive.

This Guide has also argued that the implementation of the EDD Agenda and the strategic management of the EDD Risk associated with it, will have to be moved towards the achievement of standards of EDD performance management that have been categorised in earlier chapters as being "professionalised", "excellent", "Six Sigma" or "high trust". Anything less may become unacceptable in the employment and service arenas *which, by definition, are entirely controllable and manageable.* There can be no excuses for discrimination or incidences of non-compliance. Such shortcomings are evidence of ineffective leadership; failures of governance; an impoverished, incompetent and uncaring management; and the incurring of avoidable and unnecessary costs. They represent a refusal of the organisation to accept its proper responsibilities towards the society from which it draws its custom or its revenues, or which it was set up to serve.

POSTSCRIPT

This chapter looked at ways in which EDD Risk might be categorised. It defined the process of EDD impact assessment and it described a variety of EDD Risk management strategies. It then looked at the potential for crises to be generated by organisational failures effectively to handle EDD Risk. The chapter (and this Short Guide) concluded by addressing the need for the proper strategic management of the formulation and implementation of the EDD Agenda and of the EDD Risk that may be associated with it.

Bibliography

Bain Report (2002) *The Future of the Fire Service – Reducing Risk, Saving Lives*.

Deal, T.E. and Kennedy, A.A. (1988) *Corporate Cultures*. Penguin.

Equality Act 2006 (UK).

Equality Act 2010 (UK).

Equality Act 2010 (UK) stammeringlaw.org.uk (Internet PD).

Equality Act 2010 (UK) Briefing – Burgess Salmon (Internet PD).

Equality Act 2010 (UK) Fact sheet – UK Government Equalities Office.

Equality and Diversity Scheme 2006–2009. Essex County Fire & Rescue Service.

Equality and Diversity Strategy 2006–2011. Law Society of Scotland.

Equality Scheme 2007–2010. Cleveland Police.

Equality Standard for Local Government. UK.

Field, T. (1996) *Bully in Sight*. Success Unlimited.

Fukuyama, F. (1995) *Trust – The Social Values and the Creation of Prosperity*. Hamish Hamilton.

George, J.M. (2000) Emotions and the Leadership: The Role of Emotional Intelligence. *Human Relations* 53(8).

Goleman, D. (2000) Leadership That Gets Results. *Harvard Business Review*, March–April.

Hamel, G. and Prahalad, C.K. (1994) *Competing for the Future*. Boston, MA: Harvard University Press.

Hofstede, G. (1980) *Cultures Consequences*. Sage.

Hofstede, G. (1991) *Cultures and Organizations*. McGraw-Hill.

Honey, G. (2010) *Reputation Risk*. Gower Publishing.

Jaques, E. (1964) *Time-Span Handbook: The Use of Time-Span of Discretion to Measure the Level of Work in Employment Roles and to Arrange an Equitable Payment Structure*. Heinemann.

Lessem, R. and Neubauer, F. (1994) *European Management Systems*. McGraw-Hill.

Lewin, J. (1951) *Field Theory in Social Science*. Harper & Row.

Linklater, M. (2009) The illness that dare not speak its name. *The Times*, 16 September.

MacPherson Report (1999) The Stephen Lawrence Inquiry. Sir William MacPherson of Cluny, Cm 4262–I.

Morden, A.R. (2004) *Principles of Management*. 2nd edition. Ashgate.

Morden, A.R. (2007) *Principles of Strategic Management*. 3rd edition. Ashgate.

Morden, A.R. (2009) *The Equality, Diversity and Discrimination Agenda: Change and Challenge Ahead*. The Online Journal of the Law Society of Scotland, November 2010.

Royal College of Nursing (2008) Publication code 003 292.

Sanghera, J. (2007) *Shame*. Hodder & Stoughton.

Sanghera, J. (2009) *Daughters of Shame*. Hodder & Stoughton.

The Fire and Rescue Service Review (2006) House of Commons Communities and Local Government Select Committee. HC 872–1.

Index

Lightning Source UK Ltd.
Milton Keynes UK
UKHW020321301220
375881UK00008B/71